Understanding Your Place in

GOD'S KINGDOM

Understanding Your Place in

GOD'S
KINGDOM

Your Original Purpose for Existence

MYLES MUNROE

Destiny Image. Publishers, Inc.
P.O. Box 310
Shippensburg, PA 17257-0310
"Promoting Inspired Lives."

Bahamas Faith Ministry
P.O. Box N9583
Nassau, Bahamas

Originally Published as *Kingdom Principles*
© Copyright 2006 — Myles Munroe
ISBN 13: 978-0-7684-2398-3

And as *Kingdom Principles Devotional Journal*
© Copyright 2008 — Myles Munroe
ISBN 13: 978-0-7684-2664-9

This book and all other Destiny Image, Revival Press, MercyPlace, Fresh Bread, Destiny Image Fiction, and Treasure House books are available at Christian bookstores and distributors worldwide.

For a U.S. bookstore nearest you, call: 1-800-722-6774.

For more information on foreign distributors, call: 717-532-3040.

Or reach us on the Internet: www.destinyimage.com

ISBN 13 TP: 978-0-7684-4065-2
ISBN 13 Ebook: 978-0-7684-8897-5

For worldwide distribution, Printed in the U.S.A.

1 2 3 4 5 6 7 8 9 10 11 / 14 13 12 11

Table of Contents

Devotional Journal Contents

Preface

While writing this book, I have at some time privately pondered the following questions:

1. Why is there so much hatred in the world?

2. Why do we discriminate against people who possess human value?

3. Why is there racism in the world?

4. What are the benefits of war?

5. Why do men in every generation pursue power at the expense of peace?

6. Why are there so many religions?

7. Why do the religions conflict?

8. Why can't we love one another on earth?

9. Why is no one religion good enough for all men?

10. What can I do to make a difference in this world?

11. Why is there always tension between politics and religion?

12. Will there ever be global peace and harmony on earth?

13. Why has man's scientific and intellectual advancement not been able to solve his social, cultural, and religious problems?

14. Is there hope for our world?

15. What about the future for our children? What kind of world will they live in?

Simply asking these questions can ignite a spirit of depression and despair because they expose the deficiencies and defects of humanity and cast a somber cloud of doubt about our achievements as a race as well as our potential to improve our lot.

However, I wish to declare with positive hope and excitement that this book presents the solution—an idea that is older than time yet as fresh as tomorrow in addressing the heart cries of humanity in our search for a better world. This solution is not found in religion or politics but in an idea that has been misunderstood for six thousand years—a concept that was established at the foundation of creation but then was lost. It is an idea that provides for the value, equality, significance, and purpose for each of the over six billion humans on this planet, all of whom deserve the best in life. This idea is about you and me and something that was always ours by divine right. It is a beautiful idea that has been lying dormant for centuries awaiting our rediscovery.

This book is about your original purpose for existence and the source of meaning behind your life. In these pages you will discover the Creator's divine motivation, design, and mandate for His creation and your role in that creation. After reading this book, you will be equipped with the knowledge to answer some of the questions listed above. I am convinced also that you will come to believe, as I do, that there is hope for mankind, but only as we reconnect to the source of creation and our Creator's original concepts for life on planet earth.

Moses, the great freedom fighter and former prince of Egypt, first recorded this idea 3,500 years ago in his writings, documenting the creation narrative. But it was already an ancient concept even in his day. Then, 2,000 years ago, this wonderful idea was reintroduced by a young country teacher from Galilee but later was misunderstood and lost in the complicated formation of another religion.

What is this idea? The Kingdom!

When one hears the word *kingdom*, immediately many different ideas, concepts, and pictures come to mind. Most of our concepts in life are the result of our culture, social development, and formal and informal education. We are products of our culture and interpret the world through our mental conditioning.

The concept of *kingdom* in its original and pure sense has been lost to our modern world. Kingdom as a concept does not exist anymore in the minds of people in Western civilization, particularly in the past few generations, because all the prototypes either have been destroyed or abandoned. Because there are no kingdoms or remnants of kingdoms left in the western world, we live in a generation where the true meaning of the greatest message ever told cannot be fully understood.

It is this concern that this book will attempt to address. The goal of this book is to reintroduce the concepts, principles, and nature of true authentic kingdoms as presented by the Creator and show the superior and advantageous nature of kingdom as compared to any religion, political ideology, government system, or social program. Join me as we explore and understand the precepts and principles of "the Kingdom."

Introduction

The greatest threat to civil society is mankind. Every day the flood of images on our television screens tells the sad story. Blood, death, diplomacy, conflict, hatred, fear, poverty, starvation, rape, genocide, refugees and human migration, natural disasters, daily bombings, economic uncertainty, immigration, corporate corruption, moral decay, sexual revolution, and clash of counter cultures—all of these testify to the undeniable fact that we are our own worst enemy.

All of our universities, cyber-space technology, blackberries, think tanks, G-8 meetings, fiscal and immigration policies, medical advancements, social experiments, religious conferences, peace marches, and declarations of cease-fire and peace on earth all seem to collapse at the mercy of our own self-imposed destructive spirit. We build buildings and then bomb them; we make weapons and then use them on ourselves; we invent medicines that heal and then withhold them from the sick; we improve the World Wide Web to enhance global communication and then use it to destroy the moral fiber of our children. We are our own greatest enemy.

The Source of Religion

All of this is compounded by our establishment of sophisticated religions into which we retreat to escape the social chaos we have created. Religion is the most powerful force on earth. Despite the claims of many to the contrary, everyone on earth is religious. Religion is defined as the adherence to a set of beliefs that regulate the moral, social, and ritualistic behavior of the individual. This definition would include the so-called atheist, secularist, communist, socialist, humanist or agnostic, for they all adhere to a belief system of some kind, even if it is the belief that there is no providential component in creation or life as we know it, or a belief in the power of the human as the supreme measure of truth and right.

Virtually every major problem in history and in our contemporary world can be traced to some religious foundation. Religion has motivated the massacre of millions over the years in such horrific events as the Crusades, the Inquisition, and wars related to the Protestant Reformation and the Catholic Counterreformation. Slavery, ethnic cleansing, apartheid, segregation, racial discrimination, and other oppressive practices all have been justified by some religious code or system.

Even this new millennium commenced with definitive acts of religious terrorism. The terrorist attacks of September 11, 2001 sent shock waves through the global nervous system of mankind and continues today to fuel the fires of conflict, hatred, fear, and murder throughout the world. How ironic it is that religion, the very thing that by its nature is supposed to provide the solution to mankind's problems and provide hope and faith for life, has itself created more problems throughout history than it has solved.

Perhaps this is one reason so many millions have turned away from all forms of institutionalized religions and opted to embrace such philosophies as humanism, communism, and agnosticism. Some have simply given up and lost all hope in humanity. I myself have struggled long to come to grips with this dichotomy of human nature—our desire to worship and serve some deity that we claim to be benevolent and loving, while at the same time demonstrating a destructive zeal motivated by our "allegiance" to this same deity. Along the way I too lost faith in the concept of religion and in a real sense had to seek for something beyond and superior to these defective practices created by man.

Yet religion is a natural phenomenon that exists in some form in every human culture—and always has. Primitive and modern human societies alike manifest religious rituals that define their culture and communal life. This raises the natural question: What is the source of religion, and why is it such a natural, inherent characteristic of the human spirit?

Thirty-five years of research and personal exploration of this question have led me to the conclusion that religion is the result of an inherent hunger in the human spirit that man cannot define yet must seek to satisfy. This indefinable hunger, arising from a vacuum created by the loss of something man used to possess, drives him to pursue answers beyond his own realm. Generations of humans have attempted to satisfy this hunger through superstitions, sophisticated rituals, customs, and practices that often seem to defy human logic and reason. Most human religious activities attempt to deal with the questions of mankind's existence and purpose as well as life after death and the unknown spiritual world. Many of these religions are attractive because they promise their adherents power to control the circumstances of their daily lives. Whether or not they can deliver on this promise is another matter.

The purpose of this book is to help you address these questions and to present to you a proposition that goes beyond religion straight to the heart of mankind's greatest need and offers a solution to this universal human search. I am convinced that every person on earth ultimately is searching for two things in life: *power* and *purpose*. All of us look for *meaning for our existence* and the *power* to control our lives and our circumstances; power to determine the future and predict the unknown; power over death and life. We seek this purpose and power in many ways: religion, politics, money, fame, notoriety, recognition, influence. Our pursuit of purpose and power is the primary source and motivation for the development of religion.

All Religions are the Same

All religions are the same in the sense that they attempt to answer the questions of power and meaning. They all promise power to control life and circumstances and to explain life and death. They all claim to have the truth. They all claim superiority over each other. They all compare and compete with each other. They all demand adherence to their particular belief system while denying the others. They all are motivated by contention and usually thrive in an isolated culture that excludes other segments of humanity. In fact, all religions seem to glory in a spirit of segregation and separatism. Rather than uniting humanity with common power and knowledge of purpose, religion has proven itself instead to be the great divider of mankind.

The Nonreligious Answer

This is not a religious book but a book about a concept that was introduced at the beginning of the creation of man. That concept is the source of the human search, and its absence is the reason why man "invented" religion. Before I can attempt to discuss this dynamic concept, it is necessary to refer to the document where it was first introduced. In the "book of beginnings," the first book of Moses, the great Hebrew writer and freedom fighter, these words explain the reason for mankind's search for purpose and power:

> *Then God said, "Let Us make man in Our image, according to Our likeness; let them have **dominion** over the fish of the sea, over the birds of the air, and over the cattle, over all the earth and over every creeping thing that creeps on the earth"* (Genesis 1:26 NKJV, emphasis added).

This statement documents the most important declaration ever made regarding mankind. It declares the motivation, nature, purpose, and mandate behind mankind's creation. As this statement makes clear, *dominion* is the purpose for man's creation and existence. The word "dominion" here translates the Hebrew word *mamlakah*, which can also be translated as "kingdom," "sovereign rule," or "royal power." In essence, mankind was created to have rulership over the earth.

The first thing man was given by his Creator was a "kingdom." This initial assignment and mandate of "kingdom" is the Creator's primary purpose and motivation for His human creatures. Dominion sets the framework for all the desires, passions, and activities of mankind and is the key to his fulfillment and personal and corporate peace. It is also the foundation and source of his need to control and rule his environment and circumstances. It is this kingdom mandate that validates man's desire for power. Power is natural to the human spirit.

The Loss of Power

Mankind's failure through disobedience to his Creator resulted in the loss of his dominion over the earth. He lost his kingdom mandate, his gift of divine power. In short, man lost his kingdom. It is important to note here that when man fell from grace, he lost a kingdom, not a religion. He lost dominion over the earth; he did not lose Heaven. Therefore, mankind's search is not for a religion or for Heaven, but for his kingdom.

This is why religion can never satisfy the deep hunger in the heart of man. Religion is itself the search. No religion can substitute for the kingdom or fill the vacuum in man's soul. The hunger of the human heart is for the lost kingdom.

The Message of the Bible

A careful and honest look at the biblical Script will reveal that the fundamental message of this greatly misunderstood Book is about a King and a Kingdom. The Bible is not primarily about a religion or rituals, but about the establishment of a kingdom rulership on this planet from the heavenly realm. It is about a divine project of governing earth from Heaven through mankind. In practical terms, the Bible is about a royal family mandated to colonize earth from Heaven.

This kingdom assignment is the priority of God the Creator and the object of mankind's inherent pursuit.

Misunderstanding Jesus

I believe no one who has ever lived has been misunderstood more than the young teacher who happened to be born, not by preference but by promise, through the line of the Old Testament Hebrew patriarch Abraham—Jesus the Christ. Misunderstanding Jesus has caused Muslims to reject Him, Hindus to suspect Him, Buddhists to ignore Him, atheists to hate Him, and agnostics to deny Him. But it just may be those who claim to represent Him the most—Christians—who have in fact misunderstood and, therefore, misrepresented Him the most.

If my last statement sounds outlandish and way off the mark to you, let me encourage you to read the rest of this book before closing your mind to this possibility. In my own life I have had to come to grips with my own personal defects related to my understanding of Jesus and His message. This book will demonstrate beyond doubt that Jesus' message, assignment, passion, and purpose were not to establish a religion of rituals and rules but rather to reintroduce a *kingdom*. Everything Jesus said and did—His prayers, teachings, healings, and miracles—was focused on a kingdom, not a religion. Jesus was preoccupied with the Kingdom; it was His top priority, His heavenly mandate.

Those to whom He came first, the Jews, misunderstood Jesus and saw Him as a rebel, a misfit, and a fanatic. In their minds He was, at best, a misguided rabbinical teacher spreading heresies that contaminated the teachings and laws of Moses and Judaism. In truth, they had reduced the message of Moses to a sophisticated religion where strict observance of the laws became more important than the original purpose for those laws. And they expected Jesus to do the same. The original intent of God's mandate to Moses was not to establish a religion but a nation of people who would love, serve, and honor God—a "*royal priesthood* [and] *a holy nation*" (see 1 Pet. 2:9).

The Muslim misunderstands Him as simply another in a line of prophets who was a great teacher, a good man, and a great prophet, but who fell short and failed to deliver the finished work of redemption to mankind.

The Hindu misunderstands Him as a good teacher, a good man, and just another deity to add to their list of gods to provide a service in their need for spiritual security.

The atheist, agnostic, and humanist see him as a mere man, an historical figure, whom a group of misguided men transformed into a god and an object of worship. They acknowledge that Jesus existed but deny any of His miracles as well as His claim to divinity.

The media, scientists, and secularists see Him as fair game for investigation and criticism. They acknowledge Him as an interesting subject for arguments, theories, discussion, and debates while ignoring His divine claims and questioning His validity, integrity, and sometimes, His very existence.

Christians have misunderstood Him as the founder of a religion and have transformed His teachings and His methods into customs and His activities into rituals. Many even have reduced His message to nothing more than an escapist plan for getting to heaven and His promises as a mere fire insurance policy for escaping the pains of a tormenting hell.

And yet a simple study and review of His message and priority reveals that Jesus had only one message, one mandate, and one mission—the return of the Kingdom of Heaven to earth. From the very beginning, Jesus made it clear that the principal need of the human race, and the only solution to mankind's dilemma was the Kingdom of Heaven. His first public statements reveal this Kingdom priority:

From that time on Jesus began to preach, "Repent, for the kingdom of heaven is near" (Matthew 4:17).

Blessed are the poor in spirit, for theirs is the kingdom of heaven (Matthew 5:3).

Jesus' first announcement was the arrival of the Kingdom of Heaven. His solution to the malnourished and bankrupt human spirit was not a religion but the Kingdom of Heaven. In other words, if you are spiritually poor, only the Kingdom will satisfy and fulfill your hunger. The Kingdom is God's priority and must become our priority if we are to overcome the confusion of religions and the threat of self-destruction.

Religion versus Kingdom

The power of religion lies in its ability to serve as a substitute for the Kingdom and thus hinder mankind from pursuing the genuine answer to his dilemma. My study of the nature of religion and how it impacts the process of man's search for the Kingdom uncovered several significant truths:

Religion preoccupies man until he finds the Kingdom.

Religion is what man does until he finds the Kingdom.

Religion prepares man to leave earth; the Kingdom empowers man to dominate earth.

Religion focuses on Heaven; the Kingdom focuses on earth.

Religion is reaching up to God; the Kingdom is God coming down to man.

Religion wants to escape earth; the Kingdom impacts, influences and changes earth.

Religion seeks to take earth to Heaven; the Kingdom seeks to bring Heaven to earth.

Perhaps this is why Jesus addressed the religious leaders of His day so strongly when He said:

Woe to you, teachers of the law and Pharisees, you hypocrites! You shut the kingdom of heaven in men's faces. You yourselves do not enter, nor will you let those enter who are trying to....Woe to you, teachers of the law and Pharisees, you hypocrites! You travel over land and sea to win a single convert, and when he becomes one, you make him twice as much a son of hell as you are (Matthew 23:13,15).

Then some Pharisees and teachers of the law came to Jesus from Jerusalem and asked, "Why do Your disciples break the tradition of the elders? They don't wash their hands before they eat!" Jesus replied, "And why do you break the command of God for the sake of your tradition?" (Matthew 15:1-3).

Thus you nullify the word of God for the sake of your tradition (Matthew 15:6b).

For I tell you that unless your righteousness surpasses that of the Pharisees and the teachers of the law, you will certainly not enter the kingdom of heaven (Matthew 5:20).

Jesus said to them, "I tell you the truth, the tax collectors and the prostitutes are entering the kingdom of God ahead of you" (Matthew 21:31b).

It seems clear from these words that religion is one of the greatest obstacles to the Kingdom. Perhaps this may be cause for us all to take another look at the power of religion over our lives, culture, and society.

Back to the Kingdom

Christianity as a religion is well-known, well-established, well-studied, well-researched, well-recorded, and well-distributed; but little or nothing is known about the Kingdom. As a matter of fact, most of those trained in official institutions to understand the Christian faith and propagate its purported message graduate without ever taking a single course in Kingdom studies. Often, no such course is available. The result is that few so-called ordained ministers and priests have any formal instruction at all in any Kingdom concept. Their priority is in propagating the Christian religion rather than the message and concepts of the Kingdom of God.

This perpetuation of the Christian religion and its rituals, customs, and rites has left a great vacuum in the world that must and can be filled only by understanding the Kingdom.

In this book you will learn what a kingdom is, what it consists of, how it functions, and all the components that make a kingdom unique. You will also discover the difference between a kingdom and a religion, and how it compares with all other forms of government. You will be instructed in principles of Kingdom concepts, how they relate to your daily life and how you can appropriate Kingdom citizenship here and now. This book will help you appreciate that you cannot appropriate what you don't understand nor experience what you postpone. This is your practical guide to understanding the most important message mankind has ever received; a message the whole world desperately needs to hear. This book will equip you not only to receive that message but also to share it effectively with others.

Chapter One

The Priority
of the Kingdom

It was hot that morning—over 90 degrees—and humid. I was just five years old, and excited. The heat did not bother me because that day I was chosen to lead the school pledge and national anthem. There we all stood, over three hundred of us, in our uniforms—short brown pants, long knee socks, stiff, starched white shirts, our little neck ties—holding the Union Jack. As we pledged to honor and submit to the Queen of our kingdom, we sang the two songs that were the first ones we were required to learn from birth. Every one of us knew every word, and we sang with gusto and pride:

"God save our gracious queen, long live our noble queen, God save the queen. Send her victorious, happy and glorious, born to rule over us, God save the queen."

Next came the waving of the flag of the United Kingdom of Great Britain as our voices filled the air with the second song:

"Rule Britannia, Britannia rules the waves, Britons never, never, never shall be slaves."

It has taken me almost a lifetime to understand, appreciate, and in some ways overcome the impact of those history-making experiences of my childhood. Today I understand that what we went through in those school days illustrates the nature of kingdoms. We were in the process of being fully colonized—taught to become true subjects of a kingdom and obedient worshipers of sovereignty. We were part of a global kingdom whose culture was different than our heritage. Every day we felt the impact of a foreign kingdom.

Even today, 50 years later, the impact of that kingdom is still seen, felt, heard, and experienced in every part of our independent nation of the Bahamas. I still wear a tie in 90-degree heat; I still drink tea every day; and I still drive on the left-hand side of the street. In some ways, I suppose, I am still under the influence of that kingdom mentally. When the kingdom became our priority, its impact became a reality. This book is about another Kingdom whose flag we all should hold and another King to whom we should sing praises.

Rediscovering the Priority

The greatest secret to living effectively on earth is understanding the principle and power of priorities. Life on earth holds no greater challenge than the complicating daily demand of choosing among competing alternatives for our limited time. Our life is the sum total of all the decisions we make every day, and those decisions are determined by our priorities. How we use our time every day eventually defines our lives. Life was designed to be simple, not complicated, and the key to simplifying life is *prioritization*. Identifying the correct and right priority of life is the key to a successful and fulfilled life. So then, what is the principle and concept of priority?

Priority is defined as:

The principal thing.

Putting first things first.

Establishing the most important thing.

Primary focus.

Placing in order of importance.

Placing highest value and worth upon.

First among all others.

If our priorities determine the quality of life and dictate all of our actions and behavior, then it is essential that we understand and identify our priorities. The greatest tragedy in life is not death but life without a purpose—life with the wrong priorities. Life's greatest challenge is in knowing what to do. The greatest mistake in life is to be busy but not effective. Life's greatest failure is to be successful in the wrong assignment. Success in life is measured by the effective use of one's time.

Time is the true measure of life. In fact, time is the currency of life. How you spend your time determines the quality of your life and death. You become whatever you buy with your time. Always be aware that everything and everyone around you is vying for your time. Your time is important because your time is your life. And the key to effective use of your time is establishing correct priorities. First things first!

When your priorities are correct, you preserve and protect your life. Correct priority is the principle of progress because when you establish your priority according to your purpose and goals then your progress is guaranteed. Correct priority protects your time. When you set the right priorities, then you use your time for intentional purposes; your time is not abused or wasted. Correct priority protects your energy. Correct priority protects your talents and gifts. Correct priority protects your decisions. Correct priority protects your discipline. Correct priority simplifies your life.

Failure to establish correct priority causes you to waste your two most important commodities: your time and your energy. When your priorities are not correct, you will find yourself busy with the wrong things, majoring on the minor, doing the unnecessary, or becoming preoccupied with the unimportant. Incorrect priorities in your life will cause you to invest in the less valuable, engage in ineffective activity, and abuse your gifts and talents. Ultimately, it will cause you to forfeit purpose, which results in failure.

Why is this principle of priority so important to our discussion of the Kingdom? Because if priority is the essence of life, then we should want to know what our priority in life should be so that we can live effectively. It may surprise you to know that most of the people in the world are driven by incorrect priorities that occupy and control their entire lives. What are these priorities that master most of the human race?

The answer is perhaps found the in the work of behavioral scientist and psychologist Abraham Maslow who, after studying the motivations of human behavior, concluded that all human behavior is driven by the same basic "hierarchy of needs":

1. Water.

2. Food.

3. Clothes.

4. Housing.

5. Protection.

6. Security.

7. Preservation.

8. Self-actualization.

9. Significance.

It is important to note that Maslow listed these motivational needs in order of priority. Perhaps if we are honest, we would agree that the human rat race does indeed strive for all of these things. We go to work every day, and some even hold down two or more jobs, just to secure water, food, clothing, housing, and protection. What a tragedy, to think that the basic priority driving most humans is that of simple survival!

Would it surprise you to learn that most religions are built around the promise to meet these very same needs as a priority? Meeting human needs is the premise of all religions. One common denominator of all religions is the effort to please or appease some deity in order to secure basic needs such as a good harvest, favorable weather, and protection from enemies, etc. Another factor that all religions have in common is that their primary focus is on the needs of the worshiper. Priority in religious prayers and petitions is for personal needs. Human needs drive religion. Much of what we call "faith" is nothing more than striving for the very things on Maslow's list.

The Priority of God

God established His priority at the beginning of creation and made it clear by His own declaration to mankind. Jesus Christ came to earth and reestablished God's number-one priority. Should it surprise us to discover that God's priority for mankind is completely opposite to man's priorities? Let us read God's priority for mankind as stated by the Lord Jesus. During His first discourse introducing His mission and primary message, Jesus established God's priority for all mankind with several powerful and straightforward statements:

> *Therefore I tell you, do not worry about your life, what you will eat or drink; or about your body, what you will wear. Is not life more important than food, and the body more important than clothes?* (Matthew 6:25).

Notice that this statement directly challenges Maslow's hierarchy of needs and contradicts its order. Jesus' statement also exposes man's defective priority and confirms our preoccupation with the less important. His admonition to us not to worry implies that these basic needs for maintenance should not be the primary motivator for human action. The word worry means to consume in thought, to establish as our first interest, mental preoccupation, priority concern, fretting, fear of the unknown, and to rehearse the future over which we have no control.

Continuing on, Jesus says:

Look at the birds of the air; they do not sow or reap or store away in barns, and yet your heavenly Father feeds them. Are you not much more valuable than they? Who of you by worrying can add a single hour to his life? (Matthew 6:26-27).

This statement implies that our self-worth is more important than our basic needs and should never be sacrificed for the sake of those needs.

And why do you worry about clothes? See how the lilies of the field grow. They do not labor or spin. Yet I tell you that not even Solomon in all his splendor was dressed like one of these. If that is how God clothes the grass of the field, which is here today and tomorrow is thrown into the fire, will He not much more clothe you, O you of little faith? (Matthew 6:28-30).

The thrust of these verses is that our confidence in our Creator's obligation and commitment to sustain His creation should lead us to transfer our priority from our basic human needs to the priority of cultivating and maintaining a healthy relationship with His Kingdom and with Himself.

So do not worry, saying, "What shall we eat?" or "What shall we drink?" or "What shall we wear?" For the pagans run after all these things, and your heavenly Father knows that you need them (Matthew 6:31-32).

The word "pagans" here implies that religion should not be motivated by the base drives of human needs for food, water, clothing, shelter, and the like.

But seek first His kingdom and His righteousness, and all these things will be given to you as well (Matthew 6:33, emphasis added).

Here Jesus states God's number-one priority: *Seek first His Kingdom.*

This is the most important statement made by the Lord Jesus, and it establishes what should be the first priority in our lives. Jesus identifies the Kingdom as being more important than food, water, clothing, shelter, and every other basic human need. According to His assessment, then, what should be mankind's priority and primary preoccupation in life? The Kingdom of God. God's number-one priority for mankind is that we discover, understand, and enter the Kingdom of Heaven. It is this priority that motivated me to write this book. The priority of all human beings is concealed in the words, *"Seek first the kingdom of God and His righteousness, and everything you need for life will be added to you."*

This declaration by Jesus also suggests that there must be something about the Kingdom that all of mankind has missed and misunderstood. If everything we pursue and strive for to live and survive are found in the Kingdom, then we have been misguided and perhaps have imposed on ourselves unnecessary hardship, stress, and frustration.

> *Therefore do not worry about tomorrow, for tomorrow will worry about itself. Each day has enough trouble of its own* (Matthew 6:34).

God's Priority Assignment for Mankind

For the last 35 years this simple mandate laid down by Jesus Christ has been my life's mission. And it continues to regulate my life decisions today. The benefits that have come from this commitment have been beyond my expectations, which is one reason why I am wholeheartedly committed to assisting you in understanding this wonderful reality of Kingdom living. Below I have laid out the practical process of fulfilling this mandate so that you can see clearly that this is one priority we must reorder.

Our first instruction from Jesus is to seek. This means to pursue, study, explore, understand, learn, and consider. Seekers must have a desire to know, and possess a passion for the object of their search. To seek means to give diligent dedication to and to preoccupy one's self with that which one is seeking. The Kingdom must be pursued, studied, understood, and learned.

Second, Jesus tells us to make the Kingdom *first*. In other words, the Kingdom must be our top priority, the principal thing to place before all others as most important. We must place the highest value on the Kingdom of God, setting it above everything as our primary focus. The Kingdom must be placed above everything else and should have no competition. It must be our highest priority.

Jesus then instructs us to seek first the *Kingdom*. This is the most important aspect of the mandate and must be carefully considered. First, it is important to understand that because a kingdom is not a religion, the priority of mankind should not be to seek a religion or some form of ritual. The word for "kingdom" in this verse is *basileia* (NT: 923), the Greek equivalent of the Hebrew *mamlakah* (OT: 4467), translated in Genesis 1:26 as "dominion." Both words mean dominion, sovereign rule, kingdom, reign, or royal power. In this book, we will focus on this concept in detail because it should be our priority and because it is generally an unknown or misunderstood concept in most modern cultures.

In practical terms, a kingdom may be defined as "the sovereign rule of a king over territory (domain), impacting it with his will, purpose, and intent." In this biblical text, the word "kingdom" as used by Jesus refers to God's government, God's rulership, God's dominion over the earth. The Kingdom of God means God's will executed, Gods' jurisdiction, Heaven's influence, God's administration, and God's impact and influence.

In this book, we will use the following working definition:

A kingdom is...

The governing influence of a king over his territory, impacting it with his personal will, purpose, and intent, producing a culture, values, morals, and lifestyle that reflect the king's desires and nature for his citizens.

Jesus' final instruction to us in this verse is to seek also the righteousness of the Kingdom. This is another vitally important concept that has been diluted in the waters of religion and must be recovered if we are to understand the Kingdom and experience the abundant life all humans deserve. The word *righteousness* is actually from the discipline of law, not religion, and implies right positioning. To be righteous means to be in alignment with authority, to be in right standing with authority, to have correct fellowship with authority, to be in right relationship with authority, to be in legal or lawful alignment, and to be in correct standing with the law or regulations (principles) of and to fulfill the requirements of authority.

In essence, righteousness describes the maintenance of the rightly aligned relationship with a governing authority so as to qualify for the right to receive governmental privileges. This is why Jesus emphasizes the Kingdom and the need to be righteous so that you can receive "all things added unto you." This promise includes all your physical needs, all your social needs, all your emotional needs, all your psychological needs, all your financial needs, and all your security needs, as well as your need for self significance and a sense of self-worth and purpose.

Therefore, as we have seen above, God established only two priorities for mankind: *the Kingdom of God and the righteousness of God. Kingdom* refers to the governing influence of Heaven on earth and righteousness refers to right alignment and positioning with that government authority. Our highest priorities and greatest desires should be to enter the Kingdom of God and thirst for a right relationship with God's heavenly government.

> But **seek first the kingdom** of God and His righteousness, and all these things shall be added to you (Matthew 6:33 NKJV, emphasis added).

> Blessed are those who hunger and **thirst for righteousness**, for they will be filled (Matthew 5:6, emphasis added).

The Concept of Kingdom

The concept of "kingdom" was not invented by mankind but was the first form of government introduced by the Creator. This concept appears first in the Book of Genesis at the creation of man. Man's original assignment from God was a Kingdom assignment: "Let them have dominion over...the earth." God's plan for man was to extend His heavenly Kingdom (government) to the earth through the principle of *colonization*. Man's assignment was to establish the influence and culture of heaven on earth by representing the nature, values, and morality of God in the earth. In this way, God's heavenly rule would manifest itself on earth through His extended image in mankind. This was the first Kingdom: Yahweh, the King, extending His heavenly Kingdom to earth through His offspring, man. This is the wonderful story and message of the Bible—not a religion, but a royal family.

Ever since the Fall of man, he has tried to imitate this concept of kingdom; but throughout history, man's every attempt to establish a heavenly kingdom on earth has failed. This is why religious governments always fail, whether Christian, Muslim, Hindu, or any other form. It is for this reason that God Himself had to come to earth to bring the heavenly Kingdom back to this planet. The earth cannot give rise to the Kingdom of Heaven independently; the Kingdom *of* heaven must issue forth *from* heaven. Man lost a kingdom, and a kingdom is what he is looking for. Jesus came to bring the Kingdom of Heaven back to the earth, not to establish a religion. And mankind seeks not a religion but the Kingdom we lost so long ago. This is why religion cannot satisfy or fulfill man's spirit. The Kingdom of Heaven has top priority by virtue of its role in the original purpose of man's creation. As such, the Kingdom was the first form of government on earth.

Loss of a Concept

The kingdom concept as a whole has been lost to contemporary human culture, especially in the Western world. In his attempt to create the Kingdom of Heaven on earth, man has opted to design his own forms of government. But his experiments continue to fail: evil kingdoms, empires, dictators, communism, socialism, democracy...and the list goes on. The desire for righteous government burns in the heart of every human. All of us are seeking the Kingdom even if we all don't realize it.

Many historical kingdoms of the past contained several components that resemble the Kingdom of God and can be beneficial to us when studied. I was born in 1954 under a kingdom that at that time ruled the Bahamas and colonized our lives. This experience has made it easier for me to understand the Bible because it is a book about a King and a Kingdom.

My goal in this present writing is to reintroduce the concept of the Kingdom to a world that has lost it. Most people alive today have never had any contact or relations with a kingdom. Consequently, ignorance of the kingdom concept makes it difficult to understand fully the message of the Bible. In the chapters that follow, I will unveil many of the unique concepts and components of a kingdom that will help you immediately understand the words, claims, promises, and methods of God as well as the life and message of Jesus.

According to Jesus, the most important priority and preoccupation of all mankind should be the seeking and studying of the heavenly Kingdom government and administration of the Creator God and His purposed plan and program to impact earth. But in a practical sense, how does one go about seeking this Kingdom? How does one explore the concept, nature, function, program, components, principles, and power of the Kingdom? Answering these questions is the purpose and intent of this book. To accomplish this purpose we must:

Understand kingdom concept.

Understand kingdom philosophy.

Understand kingdom government.

Understand kingdom law.

Understand kingdom culture.

Understand kingdom society.

Understand kingdom economy.

Understand kingdom citizenship.

Understand kingdom provision.

Understand kingdom worship.

Understand kingdom protocol.

Understand kingdom representation.

The secret to a full and fulfilled life is discovery, understanding, and application of the Kingdom of Heaven on earth. Religion postpones the Kingdom to a future experience. But you must remember that you cannot appropriate what you postpone. God's desire for you is that you enter the Kingdom life *now* and experience, explore, apply, practice, and enjoy living with the benefits, promises, and privileges of Heaven on earth. Let the adventure begin!

Principles

1. The greatest secret to living effectively on earth is understanding the principle and power of priorities.

2. The greatest tragedy in life is not death, but life without a purpose—life with the wrong priorities.

3. Our self-worth is more important than our basic needs and should never be sacrificed for the sake of those needs.

4. God's number-one priority for mankind is that we discover, understand, and enter the Kingdom of Heaven.

5. A kingdom is the governing influence of a king over his territory, impacting it with his personal will, purpose and intent, producing a culture, values, morals, and lifestyle that reflect the king's desires and nature for his citizens.

6. God established only two priorities for mankind: *the Kingdom of God and the righteousness of God.*

7. The concept of "kingdom" was not invented by mankind but was the first form of government introduced by the Creator.

8. Ignorance of the kingdom concept makes it difficult to understand fully the message of the Bible.

CHAPTER TWO

The Kingdom of God Versus
the Governments of Man

There is no business more serious than government.

Ninety percent of all the national and international problems facing our world today are the result either of government or religion. This includes global hunger, health epidemics, wars, terrorism, racial and ethnic conflicts, segregation, nuclear tension, and economic uncertainty.

Throughout history, man's greatest challenge has been to learn how to live in peace with himself and his neighbors. Whether it is the continent of Africa, Old Europe, Norsemen of England, the Mongols of Asia, Indians of North and South America, or the Eskimos of Iceland, tribal warfare, racial and ethnic conflicts, and full-scale war have been the human story. In all of these social and cultural expressions of humanity, the one thing that has always evolved was some kind of authority structure, a form of leadership or government mechanism to establish and maintain social order.

From the painted walls of native caves and the hieroglyphics of the tombs of ancient Egypt, to the historic pyramid structures of the Aztec worshipers, evidence abounds of man's desire and need for some form of governmental structure. The need for government and order is inherent in the human spirit and is a manifestation of a divine mandate given to mankind by the Creator. Man was created to be a governor and ruler, and therefore, it is his nature to seek some authority mechanism that would bring order to his private and social world. Government is necessary, desirable, and essential to man's social context no matter how primitive or modern. This is why man continues to search for an effective way to govern himself.

Man's need for some formal government structure is an outgrowth of his need for social order and relationship management. This need begins in the smallest prototype of society, the family, and extends all the way to the manifestation of national expressions of constitutional order. Nations need government.

The first Book of Moses, Genesis, reveals that the first prototype of government was introduced by the Creator Himself long before the first humans existed on the earth. In fact, it gives evidence of a government structure that preexisted earth and the physical universe itself. This expression of government structure was a result of a desire to bring order to chaos and productivity to emptiness.

> *Now the earth was formless [no order] and empty [chaotic emptiness], darkness was over the surface of the deep, and the Spirit of God was hovering over the waters. And God said, "Let there be light," and there was light* (Genesis 1:2-3).

Here we see that the impact of a divine, invisible, supernatural government was necessary because of disorder and chaos. Thus, the purpose for government is to maintain productive order and management. Furthermore, the creation of mankind was also a result of disorder and the need for management. A little later in Genesis we find evidence of this as one of God's motives for creating man.

When the Lord God made the earth and the heavens—and no shrub of the field had yet appeared on the earth and no plant of the field had yet sprung up, for the Lord God had not sent rain on the earth and there was no man to work [manage or administrate] the ground, but streams came up from the earth and watered the whole surface of the ground (Genesis 2:4b-6).

From these verses we see that the Creator allowed no productive growth to take place on the earth because "there was no man to work the ground." The word "work" here implies management, administration, orderly development, and making fruitful. Thus, one of the principal motives for the creation of man was to provide a manager, administrator, and ruler of the planet earth. This is why the Creator expressed it in these words:

Then God said, "Let Us make man in Our image, in Our likeness, and let them rule [or have dominion] over the fish of the sea and the birds of the air, over the livestock, over all the earth, and over all the creatures that move along the ground" (Genesis 1:26).

The mandate of the Creator for mankind was rulership and dominion. As we saw earlier, the word "dominion" here translates the Hebrew word, *mamlakah*, meaning "kingdom" or "sovereign rule" or government. Therefore, the first command given to man by his Creator was to establish a "government" on the earth to destroy chaos and to maintain order. Government is God's solution to disorder.

The logical conclusion one can derive from this scenario is, first of all, that government is God's idea; second, that the absence or lack of correct government will always lead to chaos and disorder; and third, that wherever there is chaos, disorder, or lack of productivity, the answer is correct government.

The fall of mankind as recorded in the third chapter of Genesis was the result of man declaring independence from the government of heaven, resulting in anarchy and social and spiritual chaos. Ever since that fatal fall from governing grace, man has been attempting to establish a form of self-government that would alleviate the internal and external chaos he continues to experience. Of course, that chaos is also manifested in the natural physical creation he was mandated to govern—the earth. This is the reality behind the statement of the first-century biblical writer, Paul, when he wrote:

> *The creation waits in eager expectation for the sons of God to be revealed. For the creation was subjected to frustration, not by its own choice, but by the will of the one who subjected it, in hope that the creation itself will be liberated from its bondage to decay and brought into the glorious freedom of the children of God* (Romans 8:19-21).

Paul's statement reveals the fact that government affects not only the people of the land but also the land and physical environment itself. Governing is serious business. When man rejected heaven's government, he became the source of his own governing program. The results ever since have proven that we need help. The Creator's intent was to administrate earth government from Heaven through His image (nature) in man and thus manifest His nature and character on earth. God's government is a unique structure that is yet misunderstood. I would at this point describe it as a corporate kingdom government. Government by corporate leadership! The theocratic order of a King over kings as partners in governing! This is what we would call the "Kingdom of Heaven." The kingdom government concept is God's idea.

However, when man rejected heaven's government, he had no choice but to accept as an alternative the disappointing plethora of human attempts at government. When the children of Israel left the land of Egypt, as recorded in the Exodus story, God instructed Moses to advise them that they would be governed by the laws of heaven and led by God Himself as their heavenly King on earth. This was the first step in God's plan to reinstate the Kingdom of Heaven on earth once again, using a small nation of slaves as His prototype. He expressed His divine desire through Moses, stating:

"Now if you obey Me fully and keep My covenant, then out of all nations you will be My treasured possession. Although the whole earth is Mine, you will be for Me a kingdom of priests and a holy nation." These are the words you are to speak to the Israelites (Exodus 19:5-6).

Here we see God's intent for the nation to be governed by heaven from heaven and to be an expression of His Kingdom on earth. Israel rejected theocracy, the rule of a gracious and loving King who would protect and provide for them. Instead, they substituted a king for the King. Their decision led to calamitous consequences.

The Fall of man was not the loss of heaven but rather the loss of the Kingdom government of heaven on earth. Any honest human taking a serious look at the conditions of our planet would have to conclude that earth is in need of a new, or in this case, an alternative form of government. The spiritual, social, economic, physical, environmental, and cultural conditions of our earth demand a government that is superior to any we have yet invented. Perhaps the answer to man's need for an effective and just government is found in the first official words of Jesus Christ two thousand years ago as He announced His primary mission and commented on the human condition:

From that time on Jesus began to preach, "Repent, for the kingdom of heaven is near" (Matthew 4:17).

Blessed are the poor in spirit, for theirs is the kingdom of heaven (Matthew 5:3).

Here we note that Jesus' assessment of man's spiritual and social hunger and poverty of soul can be satisfied only by receiving the Kingdom of Heaven. The Kingdom is the only source of true joy for the heart of man. Jesus' announcement identified His stated solution to man's earthly condition: *"The kingdom of heaven is near* [or 'has arrived']."

The kingdom concept originated in the mind of God and was the original governing system designed for earth. The ideal kingdom concept is unique, distinctive, and provides for the greatest benefits to its citizens.

The ideal kingdom is such a beautiful idea that only God could have thought of it. And it is the only system of governing that can bring the peace, equality, and fulfillment that mankind longs for. I use the term "ideal kingdom" concept because historically man has attempted to imitate and duplicate the heavenly design of the Kingdom with disappointing results. Man's efforts to establish kingdom government has produced defective, oppressive, and destructive models that have not only fallen short of the noble aspirations of man but has also inflicted negative repercussions on his fellowman. In essence, mankind's rejection of Heaven's Kingdom model has led to the abolition of peace and the installation of inferior forms of government. Some governments are better than others, but *all* are inferior to God's government—the Kingdom of Heaven.

The Government of Man versus the Government of God

The Bible is the most misunderstood book on planet earth, not only by those who do not prescribe to it, but also by many of those who claim to know and embrace its message. Simply stated, the Bible is about a King, a Kingdom, and a royal family of children. The Bible is not about religion and was never intended to be a religious book. Rather, its story and message are about the desire of a King to extend His Kingdom to new territories through His royal family. The Bible, therefore, is about government and governing.

What is government? Government is about order, influence, administration, distribution, protection, maintenance, accountability, responsibility. and productivity. Technically speaking, government is the person, group, or organization that executes the functions of governing. This is manifested in the exercise of authority and jurisdiction over territory and a citizenry. Government was first established by the command and mandate of God to Adam and incorporates the need to order, work, oversee, guard, and protect.

The roots of government in the western world reach back to the world of the Greeks. In Greek, *government (kubernites)* literally means to steer, to pilot, or to act as a rudder. Without law and government we have chaos. So, government is the power *given* or *derived* for the purpose of making and enforcing laws for a certain territory.

Governing incorporates the concepts of both power and authority. These two are distinct from each other and must be fully understood in order to appreciate the proper context of government. Both authority and power must be in balance for government to be successful. Authority has to do with responsibility while power has to do with ability. Authority has to do with empowerment; power focuses on exercising authority. Authority gives power its legality. Power without legitimate authority is dictatorship and inevitably results in abuse, oppression, and destruction. Authority gives power its rights.

Authority is the key to successful government. If the ruling power does not have authority, it cannot govern. The authority to govern either is given by way of a popular vote or derived by way of inherent authority. Earthly governments derive their authority from the people either through a process of choice or by usurping authority through force. For instance, a president or premier or prime minister is imbued with authority by the people who voted him or her into power.

In kingdoms, however, authority is inherent and a product of the rights of ownership. This concept is crucial in understanding the nature of kingdoms. God's authority as King is inherent. No one gives Him authority. He has authority because of who He is and because He created the earth and everything that lives on the earth. That is why Jesus could say that all authority had been given to Him. His Father had *all* authority and therefore had the right to give it to His Son. The Father had creative rights to the whole universe.

The governments of this earth get their authority by way of vote or violence. It is not inherent authority. The only government on the earth that represents inherent authority is a monarchy. A king has the power and can give it to whomever he chooses. All other governments are formed by casting a vote or by launching a revolution. In the final analysis, all human governments are substitutions for the ideal, no matter how good these governments might be. Let us take a brief look at some of man's attempts at government and structures of rulership. The most important one we will discuss will be the form of governing we call feudalism.

Feudalism

Feudalism describes a governing or ruling system that was established by virtue of the power of ownership. As a matter of fact, the authority in this system was called a "feudal lord," meaning a landowner. During the early Middle Ages, the economic and social power of societies were related to agriculture; therefore, land was the key source of power. He who owned the land owned the power. When land is power, then whoever owns the most land controls everyone and everything. This is where the idea of "real estate" originated. Landowners were the ones who were considered to possess real estate. The landowner was the "lord" of the land. Thus we find the word *landlord* used to describe those who owned land.

Therefore, the primary pursuit of all who desired power was land. Landowners were known as lords and eventually became "rulers" of their land. The more land they owned the greater their lordship, or rulership. Individuals who owned significant parcels of land became known as "kings." In other words, the prerequisite for becoming a king was the ownership of land. This is also where the idea of earthly kingdoms gets its birth. "Kingdom" was the word used to describe the territory over which a local king, or landowner, ruled or exercised ownership right and authority.

It is also important to note that because all the land was personally owned by the landlord, then private property was not possible; thus, all the people who lived on and worked the land did so at the pleasure and mercy of the king or landlord. Everything in the land, including animals, natural resources, and all other materials, were considered the personal property of the king or lord.

In many cases, where the lord or king was kind and benevolent, the people who lived, worked, and served on his land enjoyed the benefits of his kindness. And because they made his land productive and added prosperity to him, he provided, protected, and cared for them. This is why a good king tended to attract many to his kingdom. Feudalism as a concept of governing was a derivative of the original government established in the Garden of Eden under the first man, Adam, who himself was made the landlord of the earth. God's original plan was a feudal system where all men served as kings and lords of the earth, ruling not humans but the animal, plant, bird, and water kingdoms.

However, in cases where the landlord or king was not kind and merciful, the result was abuse and oppression of the people by virtue of noble status. Whoever owned the land controlled those who lived on the land. Feudalism is an illustration of the danger of putting the authority that belongs to the King of heaven into the hands of ungodly and unrighteous human kings and lords. When the culture migrated away from agriculture to industry, the noble lords eventually lost their power.

Dictatorship

Dictatorship is the form of government derived from the concept of "divine authority," which is built on the belief that certain individuals are chosen by the gods or by providence to rule the masses and exercise authority over the less fortunate or so-called "inferior" peoples. This is the form of governing we find in the biblical records and other sources such as the Egyptian pharaohs, who believed they were products of the gods and were destined to rule people by virtue of birthright.

Dictatorships have emerged in every generation and continue to do so to this day. They come in many forms and titles, but the principle and results are the same. A dictatorship is government that concentrates its power and authority in the hands of one individual who wields absolute authority unrestricted by laws, constitution, or any other social/political factor.

Dictators are considered despots and usually are driven by personal ambition or private interests. They focus in on themselves and their goals. Self-worship is also common in this form of governing. Historically, dictatorships have never succeeded for long, usually ending in tragedy and chaos. No dictatorship will survive forever. At some point, the people will revolt.

The dictatorship is also a twisted attempt by man to reestablish the original form of government established by the Creator in the Garden of Eden when He delegated total rulership and dominion control to the man. Adam was given absolute power, but the distinction was that his power and dominion were never intended to rule over other human beings but over the animal, bird, plant, and water kingdoms. Whenever the attempt is made to dominate humankind through any form of dictatorship, the natural result is rebellion and resistance. This is natural and always will be. Dictatorship over humanity is not God's original form of government.

Communism

As a form of government, communism is a combination of the first two types of governing. Communism is man's attempt to control land and people by the exercise of dictatorship. This is why a communist state repossesses all private property and attempts to enforce productivity through oppression and coercion. It seeks to accomplish this by attempting to legislate love and sharing, an approach that never succeeds because human nature cannot be forced to love or to care. These behaviors result from natural motivation and internal convictions. No law can accomplish that.

It is my view that communism is man's attempt to reestablish the Kingdom of heaven on earth as given to the first man Adam, but without the involvement of the source of creation Himself. In essence, communism is an attempt to establish a kingdom without righteousness. One can find in the writings of Marx and Engels a certain sincerity as they sought to find a way to bring power to the people (proletariat) by wresting that power from the hands of the nobility (bourgeois). It was an attempt to take ownership of land away from the nobles and put it in the hands of the people. They believed in a dictatorship of the people. Great idea? Maybe. The only problem is that government is in the hands of people. Whenever man is involved, government will fail. Communism simply exchanged power by wresting it from the hands of the czars and placing it in the hands of a new set of dictators.

Socialism

Socialism, a stepchild of communism, is another endeavor to bring the state closer to the needs of the people. It substitutes the state for the king and attempts to control society for the benefit of society. Like all the others, socialism is another failed attempt by man to govern himself. Absolute power corrupts absolutely, and the state loses its concern for the individual as it becomes more obsessed with its own power.

This leads us to our final look at man's attempt to govern himself.

Democracy

Democracy has its roots in the writings of the Greeks and is viewed by many people (even those in the Western religions) as the perfect government. Plato called it the fairest of constitutions but did so only reluctantly because he saw weaknesses within democracy that would lead to its downfall. The rule of the people, by the people, and for the people is a fine idea. It is man's attempt to get further away from despotism and tyrannical rule. Democracy as a principle is man's reaction to all the other forms of government such as feudalism, dictatorship, communism, and socialism.

A close study of the roots of western democracy will reveal that it was a reaction and rebellion against a divine choice or feudal system of governing called a kingdom. In reality, America was built on rebellion against a kingdom. The founders and framers of the American concept of governing championed the cause of democracy and adopted the Greek ideas and refined them to accommodate their aspirations. America rejected a kingdom. America's dream and guiding principles were independence, self-determination, and individuality; but while these principles serve as the bedrock of Western democracy, they remain contrary to the Kingdom principles.

Americans have never understood the potential power of a king and his kingdom because they were exposed to corrupt kings. Out of that fear they created a system of rule that would limit the power of a single man. The system of checks and balances was installed to guard against power and authority being consolidated into the hand of one individual.

This fear of totalitarianism and dictatorship is the engine that drives the motor of Western democracy, and unstably so. In the absence of the original perfect and ideal kingdom government concept, the concept of democracy is the best form of government invented by mankind and serves to protect him from his own defective nature and character. However, despite the fact that democracy is the best civil form of governing in our stressful world of demigods, democracy itself is plagued with defects that leave it wanting. The fundamental problem of democracy is its very foundation, power, and authority by majority vote.

Democracy is the best form of civil government as we know it because of its basic tenets and because of the checks and balances of the system. It is also built on the premise and principle of the "majority rule" and the protection of individual rights. Democracy has served our nations well in that it has given voice to the people and provides opportunity for broad-based participation in the political process by the people of a nation. Its checks and balances system further protects the masses from monopolization of power by one or by the few.

Despite its advantages and benefits, however, democracy does come with a few crucial defects. One such defect is its fundamental and major principle of "majority rule." This defect is critical because even though it gives power to the majority of the people, at the same time it places morality, values, and the standards for law at the mercy of the majority vote, thus legitimizing the majority's values, desires, beliefs, aspirations, and preferences.

If the power of democracy is in the people, then "we the people" become the sovereign of our lives and corporate destiny, and thus become our own providential ruler and god. This is the reemergence and manifestation of the age-old philosophy of humanism. Humanism is simply man becoming his own measure for morality, judgment, and justice that places man at the mercy of himself. So no matter how educated man may become, he can lead himself only as far as he goes himself. The record of history and the present state of the world gives evidence that man left to himself makes a poor god. Therefore, democracy without accountability to one greater than the people is an exercise in moral roulette. Simply put, democracy without God is man's worship and elevation of himself and his own intelligence. What a tragedy!

Democracy cannot succeed without God any more than communism can succeed without God. God is not subject to our politics, nor can He be, but He has created His own political system and governmental structure which, as this book will demonstrate, is far superior to all forms of earthly government. From the Creator's perspective, life *is* politics, and He is the essence of life. In Him there is no distinction between government and spirituality. They are one and the same. The assignment given to the first man in the Garden of Eden was a political assignment given to a spirit being living in a flesh body. Therefore, in the context of the original biblical mandate, the concept of the separation of church and state or religion and government is a lofty idea that has no root in biblical logic or fact. The original biblical mandate provides no foundation for it.

Everyone is religious in the sense that they bring to life their moral convictions no matter what their religious claim. We all are political *and* religious. There can be no separation. You cannot legislate a dichotomy between a man and his belief system. Legislation itself is the result and manifestation of a belief system and moral judgment. Therefore, democracy can succeed only where there is a clear accountability to a moral code accepted by the majority as being good, civil, and right, and which serves as the anchor and foundation for national governance.

In my country, the Bahamas, that moral code is recognized constitutionally and nationally as the biblical principles of the historic Judaic-Christian faith and the God of those Scriptures. This is stated within the constitutional document and provides an authoritative reference for governing within our nation. Consequently, when the majority votes and the results are in keeping with the natural laws and standards established in the biblical text, the vote is then considered legitimate. On the other hand, when the majority votes in violation of natural law and of the principles established by the biblical text, that vote or legislation becomes illegitimate.

In essence, the problem with democracy—rule of the people—is that the vote of many can be the wrong vote. Another weakness of democracy is that it is not absolute. Its concepts and laws can blow like the wind. It can be easily influenced by the changing culture. Because the citizens can be so easily manipulated by a shift in the culture and by the will of people at the top, they can be induced to abandon their rights and transfer them to those who rule over them.

Plato knew that eventually the rule of the people would deteriorate into the rule of the state. I predict with great sadness that even democracy, with all of its promises and aspirations for a good, civil, and just society, will not survive as a human government. When your best is not good enough, the only alternative is to look elsewhere for something better. There is a better alternative…and that is the heart of this book.

The Return of the King and His Kingdom

What is this alternative? It is to return to the original governing concept of God the Creator, which is the kingdom concept. Of course, people who have lived in the context of a democracy or a republic all their lives usually find it not only difficult but almost impossible to understand or accept easily this concept of a kingdom. Compounding the problem is the historical educational process that paints the concept of kingdoms in a negative light due to experiences with corrupt kings and kingdoms in the past.

As a matter of fact, to many people, in their limited understanding, a kingdom is simply a dictatorship in the hands of a family. If this is true, then the message of Jesus Christ 2,000 years ago was the promotion and establishment of a dictatorship with Himself as the dictator. He called Himself a "King" and said He came to bring back to earth a "Kingdom." According to this message, which was the only one He preached, the ultimate key to successful human earthly government is the restoration of a King and a Kingdom on earth, albeit a righteous, benevolent and good King. There is only One who can fit that role. It is the One who created us and designed each one of us with a unique purpose. We must bring back the King. This King cares for His citizens. His rule is a righteous rule.

It is this ideal, original kingdom that the heart of all humanity seeks. All of mankind throughout history, and still today, is searching desperately to find that perfect kingdom. Man has tried every imaginable way to create a flawless government. What he has failed to understand is that the original Kingdom, established by the King, is what he has been searching for all along. The kingdoms of this world must accept the Kingdom of the Lord and of His Christ. The original and ideal King and Kingdom are superior to all other forms of government. This book will prove that point as we continue our journey to understand this majestic concept.

Even within the Church we argue over government, not knowing that there is only one government. We must come to understand the superiority of a kingdom over all other forms of government.

The world needs a benevolent King. We have that King; we just don't recognize Him. I said earlier that one qualification of a legitimate king is ownership of land, which automatically makes him a lord. God, who has revealed Himself in Jesus Christ, is the ultimate Lord and owner of all things. Who makes God to be King and Lord? Nobody! He is King and Lord by right of creation. Creative rights give Him incontestable ownership rights to earth and the universe. He created all things and that automatically makes Him Lord of all. We don't give God the earth. He doesn't need us to make Him King. We can only acknowledge Him as King. His original purpose and plan was to extend His invisible Kingdom of Heaven to earth through His offspring in His image—mankind—and to rule through man as a heavenly agency. In essence, with God's Kingdom on earth, His territory, through all mankind, we would be rulers under the Ruler.

Once we are under the rule of this gracious, merciful, benevolent, loving, caring King, He takes personal responsibility for us, not as servants or serfs, but as family and royal children. This care of the citizens by the king is a concept called "kingdom welfare" and describes the king's personal commitment to look after the needs and wants of his citizens within his land. Therefore, the word *welfare* is a concept that can only be understood fully in the context of a kingdom. Whenever we submit to a king and his kingdom, we come under His welfare. Welfare is not a word that can be used in a democracy.

For many, the very word *welfare* paints negative pictures in their minds, and they believe it to be a societal curse. In the context of a kingdom, however, *welfare* is a beautiful word and describes something to be highly desired. It is a word that is used to express a king's commitment to his citizenry. This is why in all true kingdoms the concept of prosperity and national social services is called "common wealth." Again, this concept can only be understood within the concept of a kingdom. In any of the other forms of government, no regime or person has ever been successful in effectively caring for "all" of the citizens.

As a matter of fact, even under the best form of human government, democracy, there is the plight of the rich versus the poor, the have's compared to the have not's, the extreme and unequal distribution of wealth, discrimination, racism, divisions, social classifications, and ethnic segregation. History continually fails to show us a government that manifests the equality, harmony, stability, and community that man has desired and sought after from the day of the fall of Adam. Even our best is defective. No government has been able to take care of its people equally. In a true ideal kingdom, however, all the citizens' welfare is the personal responsibility of the king. This is why the original kingdom concept, as in the Kingdom of God taught by Jesus Christ, is superior to all other governments.

Therefore, in a kingdom, the concept of "commonwealth" is also very important, and the word correctly describes the nature of the relationship the king has with his citizens and subjects. The wealth in a kingdom is common. Therefore, in a true ideal kingdom there is no discrimination or distinction between the rich and the poor, for in such a kingdom all citizens have equal access to kingdom wealth and resources provided by the benevolent king. In essence, the King's interest is the welfare of the Kingdom and everything in it.

If none of the human systems of government are adequate, how then do we adopt God's original kingdom concept into our world? It begins by understanding the kingdom concept of *colonization.*

Principles

1. Ninety percent of all the national and international problems facing our world today are the result either of government or religion.

2. The need for government and order is inherent in the human spirit and is a manifestation of a divine mandate given to mankind by the Creator.

3. Man's need for some formal government structure is an outgrowth of his need for social order and relationship management.

4. The mandate of the Creator for mankind was rulership and dominion.

5. Some governments are better than others, but *all* are inferior to God's government—the Kingdom of Heaven.

6. Feudalism as a concept of governing was a derivative of the original government established in the Garden of Eden under the first man, Adam, who himself was made the landlord of the earth.

7. Feudalism is an illustration of the danger of putting the authority that belongs to the King of Heaven into the hands of ungodly and unrighteous human kings and lords.

8. A dictatorship is a government that concentrates its power and authority in the hands of one individual who wields absolute authority unrestricted by laws, constitution, or any other social/political factor.

9. Communism is man's attempt to control land and people by the exercise of dictatorship.

10. Communism is an attempt to establish a kingdom without righteousness.

11. Socialism substitutes the state for the king and attempts to control society for the benefit of society.

12. Democracy is the best form of civil government as we know it because of its basic tenets and because of the checks and balances of the system.

13. One major defect of democracy is its fundamental principle of "majority rule," which even though it gives power to the majority of the people, places morality, values, and the standards for law at the mercy of the majority, thus legitimizing the majority's values, desires, beliefs, aspirations, and preferences.

14. Our best alternative is to return to the original governing concept of God the Creator, which is the kingdom concept.

CHAPTER THREE

The Original Kingdom Concept: Colonization of Earth

From our discussions thus far, two things at least should be perfectly clear at this point. First, every person on earth, without exception, is seeking a kingdom. Consciously or unconsciously, every human activity and endeavor is directed in one way or another toward this pursuit. And second, as we have just seen, the kingdom concept of government, the original and first governmental concept, is far superior to any governmental system devised by man. The caveat, of course, is that such a kingdom be ruled by a righteous and benevolent king. Otherwise, a kingdom will prove to be no better than any other system.

The inherent superiority of a kingdom over other systems of government is an especially difficult concept for many people in the west. As I stated earlier, few westerners have ever lived under a kingdom and thus know little or nothing of how one operates. This difficulty is even more acute for citizens of the United States whose nation, after all, was established in rebellion against a kingdom.

Nevertheless, a kingdom ruled by a sovereign, righteous, and benevolent king remains the best system of government humanity could ever hope for. The reason is simple: *The kingdom concept is of heavenly, not earthly, origin.* Its appearance on earth is due to another concept that originated in heaven—the concept of *colonization.*

Simply stated, *colonization is Heaven's system for earthly influence.*

Seeing the Big Picture

In order to understand this, it is important to look at the big picture.

We humans, divided as we are by religion, ethnicity, geography, national identity, and differing governmental systems and economies, have trouble grasping the overall picture that we are one global village. Religious and cultural differences and territorial loyalties often prevent us from seeing how much we truly have in common with one another. At heart, we all share the same fears, hopes, dreams, and longings. We all share a common desire to be able to control the circumstances of our lives. Consciously or not, we all are searching for a kingdom in which all are equal, enjoying the same rights, benefits, liberty, security, health, and abundance—lives with meaning and purpose and fulfilled potential.

In the midst of our myopic pursuit of self-advancement, we fail to recognize that such a kingdom is available for the having. But we will never see it until we step back to take in the big picture.

When I studied art in college, one of the fundamental concepts I learned is always to see the end first and then work my way back. In other words, a good artist sees the finished product in his or her mind before beginning to paint or sculpt or draw. That is what it means to get the big picture—to see the end from the beginning and keep that end clearly in view throughout the creative process. Only then can the artist ensure that the finished product conforms to his or her original vision or design.

A casual observer of any given phase of the process often cannot make any sense out of it because he or she lacks the big picture of the finished product that is in the mind of the artist. A few brush strokes on a canvas may mean nothing to someone watching the painter, but a good artist will know exactly what he is doing. He will know exactly where he is going and how to get there because he already sees the end result in his mind. He sees the big picture. That is why you should never judge an artist while he is working. It is only in the finished product where his full vision and intent can be seen.

Whether you are painting a picture, carving a sculpture, or building a house, it is critical to keep the big picture—the finished product—clearly in view. Otherwise, your original dream or vision will never be realized, and you will end up with something quite different from what you intended.

The biggest problem in our world today, including the religious world, is that we are so preoccupied with the phases that we cannot see the big picture. We are so caught up with our own little part—and with fighting and arguing with everybody else over their little part—that we have lost sight of our purpose. The most important thing in life is the big picture. But all we have are snapshots. Somewhere along the way humanity lost the big picture of our purpose, and all we were left with were tiny snapshots that provide only a narrow and very misleading impression of the whole. Long ago we lost the end of our existence. Now all we have to work with are disconnected means—futile pursuits with no significance.

Purpose defines the big picture. In other words, the big picture is the original purpose or intent of the artist or builder—the desired end result. What was God's purpose as the Artist who created humanity? What was the end result He desired? As Designer of the human race, what was God's original intent? This is a critical issue for us because without purpose, human life has no meaning or significance. And that is exactly what the philosophers of our day are saying: Human life has no purpose or significance, so each of us must create or derive meaning for our lives wherever we can find it. We have lost the big picture—God's original intent for mankind—and without it our lives are nothing more than disjointed phases that make no sense.

If our lives are to have meaning, we must recover the big picture of God's original intent for us. In the beginning, God undertook a wonderful building project called the human race. Why? God's original purpose in creating mankind—His big picture—was to extend His invisible rulership to the visible world. He wanted to extend His heavenly country to another territory. His desire, then, was to establish on earth a *colony of Heaven.*

God's Big Picture

Colonization as a concept was not invented by man. It is not the product of any human kingdom or culture. Colonization originated in the mind of God. It was His idea. God's original purpose was to establish a manifestation of His heavenly Kingdom on earth without coming to earth Himself.

A colonizing authority, such as a king, does not have to be present physically for colonization to occur. The mere presence of the *influence* of that authority is sufficient. As long as God could extend His kingly governing authority over the earth through delegated representatives, His influence would hold sway here without the necessity of His physical presence.

God's original intent was to extend His heavenly government *over* the earth, and His plan for accomplishing this was to establish a colony of heaven *on* the earth. This was God's big picture. The King of Heaven has a big agenda, bigger than national or international affairs. His is an *inter-realm* agenda. God deals with *inter-realm affairs*, the relationship between the invisible realm of Heaven and the visible realm of earth. His plan was to connect these two through colonization. However, God was not content merely to establish His influence on the earth; He wanted to take some citizens out of heaven and put them on earth to establish the colony.

How did He accomplish this? Let's examine some statements from the Bible, which is the *constitution* of the Kingdom of Heaven. Like any other constitution, the Bible lays out the laws, principles, and characteristics that define God's Kingdom. Consider first the opening words of this constitution—its "preamble":

In the beginning God created the heavens and the earth (Genesis 1:1).

This opening statement establishes God's universal kingship by divine right of creation with absolute authority to do whatever He pleases. A little further down we find earth's "colonial charter":

Then God said, "Let Us make man in Our image, in Our likeness, and let them rule over the fish of the sea and the birds of the air, over the livestock, over all the earth, and over all the creatures that move along the ground." So God created man in His own image, in the image of God He created him; male and female He created them. God blessed them and said to them, "Be fruitful and increase in number; fill the earth and subdue it. Rule over the fish of the sea and the birds of the air and over every living creature that moves on the ground" (Genesis 1:26-28).

With these words God, the King and Lord of Heaven, declared His colonial intent. This colonial charter delineated the purpose and defined the parameters of the colony. It also designated the persons who received responsibility for carrying out the King's desire.

Notice that this statement says nothing about religion. This charter is not a religious declaration; it is a government document that defines governmental intent and establishes governmental authority. So the King, in this one statement, declares His big picture—to create some beings just like Himself, place them on the earth, and let them rule it for Him as vice-regents of His heavenly government. This was His plan and His purpose for creating man. Because the purposes of God are unchanging, this is still His purpose and plan today.

Heaven's Crown Land

God created the earth as a place over which to extend His influence, but He intended to do it through mankind, not Himself. He designed man to be a fit colonizer of the physical world He wanted to colonize. That is why we humans are so well suited physically for life in this world.

The Bible says that God created man *"from the dust of the ground"* (see Gen. 2:7). Scientific evidence confirms this. Our bodies are made of the same stuff as the earth. Before God created us, He fashioned a physical world that would be a perfect environment for us to fulfill our purpose and destiny. Then He formed our physical bodies from the same material. Man is a triune being just like his Creator. We reflect His image even in our composition. Man is a spirit being after the nature and essence of his source, Father God; he lives in a body, which is his earth suit that allows him to relate to the physical environment; and he possesses a soul, which is his intellect, will, and emotional faculties. We are suited for the earth as perfectly as God is suited for Heaven.

As we discussed earlier, the foundation and qualification for kingship is rightful ownership of land. In a kingdom, the land is the personal property of the king, and it is this ownership right that designates him as lord. In a kingdom, when referring to the physical land, the territory is called "crown land." This implies the land is property of "the crown," referring to the king himself. By creative right, the earth is heaven's "crown land." In a kingdom, all the land within the kingdom belongs to the king. Every square foot of territory is his personal property—his "king-domain." In a true kingdom, therefore, there is no such thing as private property owned by the citizens; the king owns all.

The Bahamas, where I live, was once part of the United Kingdom of the British Empire. When the British seized the Bahamas from the Spanish, all 700-plus islands immediately became the personal property of the king of England. They did not become the property of the British government; there's a difference. These islands became the personal property of the British sovereign. All of us who grew up under that arrangement understood that all the land was known as crown land, meaning it belonged to the one who wore the crown. As a matter of fact, during those years, it was not uncommon for the king or queen of England to give an island as a birthday present to a son or daughter or niece or nephew. Since the islands were crown land, the monarchs, on their own prerogative, could give them away at any time to anyone they wished as personal gifts. As a matter of fact, this land could be given to any citizen as a personal gift of the government at the authority of the king, and many people in our colony received large parcels of land for personal use.

The same is true in God's Kingdom. God owns the earth and everything on it; the earth is His crown land. As an ancient poet wrote:

The earth is the Lord's, and everything in it, the world, and all who live in it; for He founded it upon the seas and established it upon the waters (Psalm 24:1-2).

Because God owns the earth, He can do with it however He pleases. And it pleased Him to give it to man. Again, in the words of the ancient poet:

The highest heavens belong to the Lord, but the earth He has given to man (Psalm 115:16).

Don't make the mistake of equating this with ownership. Crown land given to someone by the king remains crown land. At any time the king can take it back and give it to someone else. That is the king's prerogative. So when God "gave" the earth to man, He did not relinquish ownership. We possess the earth as a trust, as stewards, as "kings" under the High King of Heaven. The King gave us dominion over the earth, not as owners but as vassal-kings to extend His heavenly government to the earthly realm. He gave us rulership, not ownership. We have the privilege to rule the earth, and with that privilege also comes the responsibility of wise and righteous management. And we are accountable to the King for how we manage our domain.

It is also on this prerogative of Kingship and Lordship that God could, without the permission of its current inhabitants, promise Abraham the land of Canaan as a birthright.

Today we see this understanding of crown land applied in the nation of Israel. The ancient Jewish law handed down through Moses stipulated that no property sales in Israel were permanent because the land belonged to God:

The land must not be sold permanently, because the land is Mine and you are but aliens and My tenants. Throughout the country that you hold as a possession, you must provide for the redemption of the land (Leviticus 25:23-24).

Israelites were free to occupy their own plot of land, develop it, cultivate it, live off of it, and even pass it on to their heirs. They were not to sell it, however, especially to non-Israelites. If financial circumstances necessitated selling the property to a fellow Israelite, the law made provision for the land to be returned. Every 50 years Israel celebrated a Year of Jubilee, during which time any land that had changed hands since the previous jubilee year automatically reverted to the original possessor.

In Israel today, a similar principle is in effect. When young couples in Israel marry, the Israeli government provides or assists them with their first house. Why? Because there is no private ownership of property in Israel. Officially, the land belongs to God. The principle here is that in a kingdom, living on and using the land is a privilege, not a right.

This practice reflects a kingdom consciousness that we all need to cultivate. It is critical for our understanding of the Kingdom and how it works that we recognize that the whole earth is Heaven's crown land and that we are merely "aliens" and stewards of God's property.

God's Colonial Intent

God never does anything to no purpose. From the very beginning, God's intent for the earth was that it be colonized. Isaiah, an ancient scribe and spokesman for the King, wrote:

...He who created the heavens, He is God; He who fashioned and made the earth, He founded it; He did not create it to be empty, but formed it to be inhabited... (Isaiah 45:18).

Our presence on earth was a colonial decision by our King. He created this planet as new territory, fashioned us out of the same material, planted us here, and issued the colonial charter giving us dominion. We own nothing but have access to everything, as long as we operate within the parameters of the governing principles the King has established for His Kingdom. This is what it means to be a colony of Heaven.

The concept of colonization is the most important component of a kingdom that we must understand or else it will be impossible to fully grasp the essence of the message of the Bible, the prophets, and the focus and priority of Jesus Christ. It is the misunderstanding or ignorance of this kingdom concept of colonization that has produced all human religions and sects. Christianity as a religion is itself a product of this misunderstanding. The primary purpose, motive, plan, and program of God the Creator was to colonize earth with Heaven.

Understanding the concept of colonization is key because once we understand what God intended, we will understand what God is doing. He put people on this planet for the purpose of expanding His influence and authority from the supernatural realm to the natural realm. A colony, by definition, is populated by people who originally came from another place. It is an outpost inhabited by citizens of a faraway country whose allegiance remains with their home government. Stated another way, a colony is "a group of emigrants or their descendants who settle in a distant land but remain subject to the parent country."[1]

Colonization involves citizens of one country inhabiting foreign territory for the purpose of influencing that domain with the culture and values of their native country and governing it with the laws of their home government. For example, the message of Jesus as stated in His mission statement recorded in Matthew 4:17, "...the kingdom of heaven has arrived" (author's paraphrase), would indicate that the first colony of Heaven had returned to earth through Him. As citizens of heaven, we inhabit the earth for the purpose of influencing it with the culture and values of Heaven and bringing it under the government of the King of Heaven.

Paul of Tarsus, a first-century ambassador and colonizer for the King of heaven, described the King's colonial intent this way:

...to make plain to everyone the administration of this mystery, which for ages past was kept hidden in God, who created all things. His intent was that now, through the church, the manifold wisdom of God should be made known to the rulers and authorities in the heavenly realms, according to His eternal purpose which He accomplished in Christ Jesus our Lord (Ephesians 3:9-11).

God's intent was to plant a colony of His citizens on the earth to make His "manifold wisdom"—His heart, mind, will, and desires—known to "the rulers and authorities in the heavenly realms." In other words, to the spirit world. His purpose in colonizing earth was to show the spiritual powers of darkness how beings created in His own image could be planted on the earth and bring in the government and culture of Heaven so that in the end, the earth would look just like Heaven.

In summary:

1. A colony is a group of citizens established in a foreign territory to influence that domain for their home government.

2. A colony is a foreign territory inhabited by citizens charged to influence that domain with the culture and values of their government.

3. A colony is the presence of a distinct cultural citizenry in a foreign territory governed by the laws and culture of their home government.

Such is the concept of kingdom colonization.

Understanding Kingdom Concepts

Studying the concept of kingdoms is important for a couple of reasons. First, because most of us today, particularly in the west, have never lived in a kingdom, the concept is completely foreign to us. We simply do not know what it is like to live under a king. This might not be a problem were it not for the second reason for studying the Kingdom: *God's government, the government of Heaven, is a kingdom, and God is the King*. And because His Kingdom extends through all creation, encompassing both the supernatural and the natural realms, it covers us also, which is why we need to understand it. A third and critical reason to study and restore this concept of kingdom is because the Bible is not about a religion or an organization but a King and His Kingdom. Therefore, in order to correctly understand, interpret, and apply the Scriptures, knowledge of kingdoms is necessary.

The kingdom is the oldest of all forms of government and the only one that is of divine origin. God "invented" the kingdom concept and established it first in Heaven. Simply stated, a kingdom is simply a domain over which a king has rulership. Heaven was the first domain that God created. Although invisible, it is a very real place, even more real than what we call reality. The natural came from the supernatural; therefore, the supernatural is always more real than the natural. Heaven is more real than earth, even though we cannot see it with our physical eyes. In the beginning, God established a kingdom as the governmental system for ruling the supernatural realm of Heaven.

Once His Kingdom was established in Heaven, God desired to extend it to another realm. With this end in mind (the big picture) He created a visible, physical universe with billions of stars, including the one we call *Sol*, the sun around which revolves this planet we call Earth. The King chose this planet specifically as the location of His Kingdom colony in the natural realm. He created it for that purpose. Then He placed on it human beings created in His image to run the colony for Him. In this way, God also established the first earthly kingdom, which was merely an extension of His Kingdom in Heaven.

Through rebellion against the King, however, man lost his rulership. We have been trying to get it back ever since. Even though we lost our earthly kingdom, we still retain the original kingdom idea that the King implanted in our spirit. We are searching for the Kingdom all the time, but without God we can never find it because it is from Him.

In our Kingdom search through the ages, man has developed and experimented with many different systems of government, as we saw earlier in this chapter. Every one of them, including those we call kingdoms, are defective because mankind is defective. But they all are driven by our desire to regain and restore the original Kingdom. This is not a "utopian" fantasy. In the beginning, God established utopia in heaven—and then extended it to earth. Our utopian dreams are simply expressions of our yearning to regain the Kingdom we once had but lost.

According to the "colonial charter" stated in Genesis 1:26 that we looked at earlier, man originally was given an earthly kingdom to rule over, which was perfect. Adam and Eve were overlords of the physical domain, corulers who themselves were ruled only by God, their Creator-King. They were His people, and He was their God; there was no intermediary rulership.

Human kingdoms, which at best were but dim and flawed reflections of God's Kingdom, had citizens who were also subjects of the king, meaning that they were "subject" to the king's personal ambitions, goals, whims, and desires. God's Kingdom is different. In the Kingdom of God there are no subjects, only citizens—but every citizen is a king (or queen) in his or her own right. This is why the Bible refers to God as the "King of kings." He is the High King of Heaven who rules over the human kings He created in turn to rule over the earthly domain.

The Kingdom Is Here

Adam and Eve's rebellion cost them their kingdom. Chapter 3 of Genesis relates the sad story of how the human pair fell victim to the lies and deceptions of the serpent, which embodied the prince of darkness, that fallen angel known as satan or lucifer. With Adam and Eve's abdication, lucifer seized control of their earthly domain as a brazen, arrogant, and illegal pretender to the throne.

Immediately the King of Heaven put in motion His plan to restore what man had lost. And what did man lose? A *kingdom*. Adam and Eve did not lose a religion because they had never had a religion; they had a kingdom. So when God set out to restore what they had lost, He set out to restore a kingdom, not a religion. Religion is an invention of man, born of his efforts to find God and restore the kingdom on his own. But only God can restore the kingdom man lost.

After the disaster in Eden, the King confronted His rebellious corulers and their deceiver and addressed each one in turn. Of greatest interest to us in this context is what the King said to the serpent, because it has kingdom implications:

> *I will put enmity between you and the woman, and between your offspring and hers; He will crush your head, and you will strike His heel* (Genesis 3:15).

Referring to the woman's "offspring" by the singular pronoun "He," indicates that the King was speaking of one *specific* offspring—one who would strike a fatal blow against lucifer and his schemes by "crushing" his head. As the rest of Scripture makes abundantly clear, this one specific offspring appeared thousands of years later as the man Jesus Christ of Nazareth, who was the Son of God embodied in human flesh.

When Jesus appeared on the scene in real, space-time history, He brought a message not of a religion, new or old, but of the Kingdom:

> *From that time on Jesus began to preach, "Repent, for the kingdom of heaven is near"* (Matthew 4:17).

These are the first recorded words of Jesus. The phrase "that time" refers to the arrest of John the Baptist, a prophet whose mission was to announce the arrival of the King. Now the King Himself was on the scene, and He was announcing the arrival of the *Kingdom*. This was the only message Jesus preached. Search all four of the New Testament Gospels of Matthew, Mark, Luke, and John, and you will find that Jesus always talked about the Kingdom. Everything He said and did related to the Kingdom and its arrival on earth.

Jesus said, *"Repent"* (which means to change your mind or adopt a new way of thinking), *"for the kingdom of heaven is **near"*** (which means, in effect, that it has arrived). In other words, Jesus was saying, "Change your way of thinking! The Kingdom of Heaven is here! I brought it with me!" When Jesus brought the Kingdom of Heaven to earth, He brought also the promise of restoring to mankind the dominion over the earth that Adam and Eve had lost in Eden. He brought back our rulership.

Before we could be fully restored to our Kingdom, however, the matter of our rebellion against God had to be dealt with. This rebellion is what the Bible calls sin, and it is universal in human nature, a legacy of Adam and Eve's treason in Eden so long ago. Jesus' death on the cross paid the price for our rebellion so that we could be restored to a right standing with God, our King, and be reinstalled in our original and rightful place as rulers of the earthly domain. The "gospel" message—the "good news"—is more than the Cross. The Cross is the doorway that gets us back into the Kingdom. The Cross of Christ, therefore, is all about Kingdom restoration. It is about restoration of power and authority. It is about regaining rulership, not religion.

Sons, Not Servants

Why did God wait thousands of years from the promise in Eden of Kingdom restoration to its realization with the coming of Jesus? He had to allow the course of human history to flow until the timing was right. In order for us to understand what we lost when we lost the Kingdom, much less understand kingdom principles, God needed the right proto-type as an example. Across the millennia, many human civilizations and kingdoms rose and fell until finally a kingdom appeared that had every-thing God needed to show how His Kingdom was supposed to work. When the Roman Empire came to power, it had a concept of citizenship. It had a concept of lordship (ownership). It had a king and a domain. It practiced colonization. Rome had such an influence that wherever it advanced, that part of the world became like Rome. When God saw Rome, He said, "That's exactly what I want."

When the time was right, the King of Heaven sent His Son to restore His Kingdom on earth. Paul of Tarsus stated it this way:

> *But when the time had fully come, God sent His Son, born of a woman, born under law, to redeem those under law, that we might receive the full rights of sons* (Galatians 4:4-5).

The fullness of time has nothing to do with clocks but everything to do with seasons. When the season of history was right, when the Roman Empire had risen to serve as a living example, when everything was in place according to divine purpose, God sent His Son into the physical world with the message that the Kingdom of Heaven had arrived. What was His purpose in restoring the Kingdom? Not to give us a religion but to restore to us our "full rights" as sons and daughters of the King.

The King of Heaven wants sons and daughters, not servants. Religion produces servants. It revels in the spirit of servitude. Please don't misunderstand me. A servant heart is, as Jesus said, the key to greatness in the Kingdom of God (see Matt. 20:26-27). And He said that He Himself came to serve rather than to be served (see Matt. 20:28). But this kind of service should always proceed from the place of security in our knowledge that we are sons and daughters of the King and simply are following His example. Servanthood in the religious spirit, on the other hand, proceeds from a sense of false humility and self-deprecation where one sees oneself not as a son or daughter, but as a slave. Sons and daughters of the King see service as a *privilege*; religious people see it as an obligation. And therein lies the difference. Sons and daughters serve willingly *because* they are sons and daughters. Religious people serve grudgingly because they feel they have no choice if they hope to win the approval of the King. Never confuse ser*ving* with being a ser*vant*.

Jesus came that we might "receive the full rights of sons." This is legal language. There is not a bit of religion in these words. They refer to *legal* rights and entitlements based on relationship of birth. We are sons and daughters of God. Sonship is our right by creation. Christ did not die to improve us; He died to regain and confirm us. The price He paid in His own blood was not to make us worthy but to prove our worth. He did not come to earth to enlist an army of servants. He came to restore the King's sons and daughters to their rightful position—rulership as heirs of His Kingdom.

If we are heirs and are destined to rule in our Father's Kingdom, then we had better learn to understand His Kingdom and how it operates. We had better learn its principles and concepts. We must learn how to think, talk, and live like Kingdom citizens. The Kingdom is the most important message of our age and the answer to the dilemma of ancient and modern man. According to Jesus Christ, everyone is trying all they can to find it and forcing their way through life to lay hold on it:

Since that time, the good news of the kingdom of God is being preached, and everyone is forcing his way into it (Luke 16:16b).

Everyone of the over six billion people on earth are searching for this Kingdom. This book is to help you and your fellow planet dwellers discover and understand it. With this end in mind, the remaining chapters of this book will examine in detail key concepts of the Kingdom of Heaven.

Endnote

1. *Nelson's Illustrated Bible Dictionary*, (Nashville: Thomas Nelson Publishers, 1986).

Principles

1. Colonization is Heaven's system for earthly influence.

2. God's original intent was to extend His heavenly government over the earth, and His plan for accomplishing this was to establish a colony of Heaven on the earth.

3. By creative right, the earth is Heaven's "crown land."

4. The King gave man rulership of the earth, not ownership.

5. A colony is "a group of emigrants or their descendants who settle in a distant land but remain subject to the parent country."

6. As citizens of Heaven, we inhabit the earth for the purpose of influencing it with the culture and values of heaven and bringing it under the government of the King of Heaven.

7. God's government, the government of Heaven, is a Kingdom, and God is the King.

8. A kingdom is simply a domain over which a king has rulership.

9. In the Kingdom of God there are no subjects, only citizens—but every citizen is a king (or queen) in his or her own right.

10. When Jesus brought the Kingdom of Heaven to earth, He brought also the promise of restoring to mankind the dominion over the earth that Adam and Eve had lost in Eden.

11. The King of Heaven wants sons and daughters, not servants.

12. Jesus came that we might "receive the full rights of sons."

CHAPTER FOUR

Kingdom Concept #1: Understanding the Kingdom Concept of Kings

In recent times, it has been a popular notion to celebrate the opposition against monarchies, and many have even suggested the eradication of the concept of monarchies from our so-called modern or post-modern world. Popular uprisings against the remaining monarchies in the name of the pursuit of democracy have become the craze of today's self-proclaimed freedom fighters. In some cases it may be justifiable; in many of the instances cited, these kingdoms are filled with contradictions, abuse, oppression, social extremes, and dictatorial administrations. However, it must also be noted that many of the democracies in our world today are also plagued with the same defects and shortcomings. In essence, the problem is not the king, the kingdoms, or even the form of government, but the defects in the human nature that functions in any of these systems.

Yet the kingdom concept is the only one presented, preached, promoted, taught, and established by Jesus Christ throughout His ministry. His proposed solution to mankind's problems on the earth is the establishment of the Kingdom of Heaven in the earth. As a matter of fact, the message of the Bible and, more specifically, the focus of Jesus was not a religion or, for that matter, any of the many subjects we have magnified and many have preached as "the gospel" or good news to the world. For instance, Jesus never preached as a priority public message subjects like faith, prosperity, giving, deliverance, or even His death on the Cross or resurrection as "the gospel." But He repeatedly promoted and declared "the Kingdom of God and Heaven" as His principal message.

I am well aware that what I just said may be cause for much reaction, mental conflict, and religious resistance; but I would encourage you to search and research the four Gospels for yourself and discover this surprising reality. Jesus also indicated that this message of the "Kingdom" would be His disciples' message to their world.

Jesus' message of the Kingdom was foreshadowed in the Old Testament centuries before He was born in Bethlehem. Here are two examples. The first one indicates God's motivation for delivering the slave clans of Israel from Egyptian oppression:

> *"Now if you obey Me fully and keep My covenant, then out of all nations you will be My treasured possession. Although the whole earth is Mine, you will be for Me a kingdom of priests and a holy nation." These are the words you are to speak to the Israelites* (Exodus 19:5-6).

In the second example, we see the Old Testament Messianic promise declared by the prophet Isaiah, strongly indicating the governmental aspects of the Kingdom mandate:

> *For to us a child is born, to us a son is given, and the government will be on His shoulders. And He will be called Wonderful Counselor, Mighty God, Everlasting Father, Prince of Peace. Of the increase of His government and peace there will be no end. He will reign on David's throne and over His kingdom, establishing and upholding it with justice and righteousness from that time on*

and forever. The zeal of the Lord Almighty will accomplish this (Isaiah 9:6-7).

Jesus' message was clearly kingdom focused and not religiously motivated:

From that time on Jesus began to preach, "Repent, for the kingdom of heaven is near" (Matthew 4:17).

Jesus went throughout Galilee, teaching in their synagogues, preaching the good news of the kingdom, and healing every disease and sickness among the people (Matthew 4:23).

Blessed are the poor in spirit, for theirs is the kingdom of heaven. Blessed are those who mourn, for they will be comforted (Matthew 5:3-4).

For I tell you that unless your righteousness surpasses that of the Pharisees and the teachers of the law, you will certainly not enter the kingdom of heaven (Matthew 5:20).

Our Father in heaven, hallowed be Your name, Your kingdom come, Your will be done on earth as it is in heaven (Matthew 6:9b-10).

But seek first His kingdom and His righteousness, and all these things will be given to you as well (Matthew 6:33).

Jesus went through all the towns and villages, teaching in their synagogues, preaching the good news of the kingdom and healing every disease and sickness (Matthew 9:35).

As you go, preach this message: "The kingdom of heaven is near" (Matthew 10:7).

But if I drive out demons by the Spirit of God, then the kingdom of God has come upon you (Matthew 12:28).

He replied, "The knowledge of the secrets of the kingdom of heaven has been given to you, but not to them" (Matthew 13:11).

When anyone hears the message about the kingdom and does not understand it, the evil one comes and snatches away what was sown in his heart (Matthew 13:19a).

Jesus told them another parable: "The kingdom of heaven is like a man who sowed good seed in his field" (Matthew 13:24).

He told them another parable: "The kingdom of heaven is like a mustard seed, which a man took and planted in his field" (Matthew 13:31).

He told them still another parable: "The kingdom of heaven is like yeast that a woman took and mixed into a large amount of flour until it worked all through the dough" (Matthew 13:33).

The kingdom of heaven is like treasure hidden in a field. When a man found it, he hid it again, and then in his joy went and sold all he had and bought that field (Matthew 13:44).

Again, the kingdom of heaven is like a merchant looking for fine pearls. When he found one of great value, he went away and sold everything he had and bought it (Matthew 13:45-46).

Once again, the kingdom of heaven is like a net that was let down into the lake and caught all kinds of fish (Matthew 13:47).

I will give you the keys of the kingdom of heaven; whatever you bind on earth will be bound in heaven, and whatever you loose on earth will be loosed in heaven (Matthew 16:19).

I tell you the truth, some who are standing here will not taste death before they see the Son of Man coming in His kingdom (Matthew 16:28).

And He said: "I tell you the truth, unless you change and become like little children, you will never enter the kingdom of heaven. Therefore, whoever humbles himself like this child is the greatest in the kingdom of heaven" (Matthew 18:3-4).

Therefore, the kingdom of heaven is like a king who wanted to settle accounts with his servants (Matthew 18:23).

For the kingdom of heaven is like a landowner who went out early in the morning to hire men to work in his vineyard (Matthew 20:1).

Jesus said to them, "I tell you the truth, the tax collectors and the prostitutes are entering the kingdom of God ahead of you" (Matthew 21:31b).

The kingdom of heaven is like a king who prepared a wedding banquet for his son. He sent his servants to those who had been invited to the banquet to tell them to come, but they refused to come (Matthew 22:2-3).

Woe to you, teachers of the law and Pharisees, you hypocrites! You shut the kingdom of heaven in men's faces. You yourselves do not enter, nor will you let those enter who are trying to (Matthew 23:13).

And this gospel of the kingdom will be preached in the whole world as a testimony to all nations, and then the end will come (Matthew 24:14).

Then the King will say to those on His right, "Come, you who are blessed by My Father; take your inheritance, the kingdom prepared for you since the creation of the world" (Matthew 25:34).

After this, Jesus traveled about from one town and village to another, proclaiming the good news of the kingdom of God (Luke 8:1).

And He sent them out to preach the kingdom of God and to heal the sick (Luke 9:2).

Then He took them with Him and they withdrew by themselves to a town called Bethsaida, but the crowds learned about it and followed Him. He welcomed them and spoke to them about the kingdom of God, and healed those who needed healing (Luke 9:10b-11).

I tell you the truth, some who are standing here will not taste death before they see the kingdom of God (Luke 9:27).

Do not be afraid, little flock, for your Father has been pleased to give you the kingdom (Luke 12:32).

And I confer on you a kingdom, just as My Father conferred one on Me (Luke 22:29).

Jesus said, "My kingdom is not of this world. If it were, My servants would fight to prevent My arrest by the Jews. But now My kingdom is from another place" (John 18:36).

"You are a king, then!" said Pilate. Jesus answered, "You are right in saying I am a king. In fact, for this reason I was born, and for this I came into the world, to testify to the truth. Everyone on the side of truth listens to Me" (John 18:37).

My purpose for listing all of these statements is to show and emphasize the preoccupation Jesus had with the kingdom concept rather than a religion. Note in particular the last statement above, where Jesus declares Himself a "king" and not a president or prime minister or mayor. This is why it is necessary and essential that we rediscover and desire to understand the Kingdom as a concept and a reality. It is the foundation of God's plan for mankind.

The original ideal kingdom concept is distinct from the earthly version even though it contains many of the same components and concepts of all kingdoms. Despite the many failed kingdoms throughout history, the questions still arise: Why did God choose a kingdom and not a republic? Why did God choose a kingdom and not a democracy or socialism? What are the benefits of being in a kingdom over a democratic republic or a communistic regime? Why is a kingdom better than a democracy or socialist form of government? Why is Jesus a King and not a president?

What exactly is a kingdom? Very simply, a kingdom is the government of a king. More specifically, a kingdom is the sovereign rulership and governing influence of a king over his territory, impacting it with his will, his intent, and his purpose, manifesting a culture and society reflecting the king's nature, values, and morals. A kingdom is the governing impact of a king's will over a territory or domain, his influence over a people, and a government led by a king.

Therefore, the very heart of any kingdom is its king. This definition perfectly describes the relationship of God to the heavenly realm. Heaven exists because of the creative activity of God. Throughout its entire expanse, it is infused with His presence, character, and authority. There is no corner of heaven where His will is not accomplished. In every way God is the unrivaled and unequalled King of Heaven.

The same was true in the natural realm when God extended His Kingdom authority to the earth through the man and woman He created in His image and released to rule in His name. They rebelled against the King's authority, however, and lost their rulership. Control of the earthly realm then passed *temporarily* to a demonic usurper until the day in the King's sovereign plan when it would be restored to its rightful ruler.

In the fullness of time, Jesus came to the earth and reestablished the Kingdom. Because only a king can establish a kingdom, this act alone reveals that Jesus Christ is the King. The Bible, the constitution of the Kingdom of Heaven, leaves no doubt as to the Kingship of Jesus. Perhaps the clearest statement of all is found in the 18th chapter of the Gospel of John where Jesus, mere hours before His execution by crucifixion, has a revealing exchange with Pontius Pilate, the Roman governor of the province of Judea. Falsely arrested, illegally tried, and wrongfully condemned for "blasphemy" by the Jewish religious authorities in Jerusalem, Jesus now stands before Pilate for judgment. Pilate has heard the accusation that Jesus claims to be a king. So the governor asks Him directly:

> *"Are you the king of the Jews?"...Jesus said, "My kingdom is not of this world. If it were, My servants would fight to prevent My arrest by the Jews. But now My kingdom is from another place."*

"You are a king then!" said Pilate. Jesus answered, "You are right in saying I am a king. In fact, for this reason I was born, and for this I came into the world, to testify to the truth. Everyone on the side of truth listens to Me." "What is truth?" Pilate asked (John 18:33b,36-38a).

Jesus said, *"My kingdom is not of this world,"* and *"My kingdom is from another place,"* clearly implying that He was a King. He was speaking of the Kingdom of Heaven. Notice that Jesus said that His Kingdom was not *of* or *from* this world; He never said that it was not *in* this world. His Kingdom on earth originated in Heaven.

When Pilate pressed further, Jesus plainly said, *"I am a king."* He then said, *"I came into the world to testify to the truth."* What truth? The truth that He was a King with a Kingdom. What could be clearer than that? *Testify* is a word often used to describe what a witness does in a courtroom—testifying or avowing to what he has seen or heard. The original Greek word employed here has an even deeper meaning. It is a word of experimentation from the laboratory and means to verify or validate. Essentially, Jesus said to Pilate, "I came to earth because I am a King, and I will prove it by putting it to the test. I testify to the truth that a King is here, a Kingdom is here, and this Kingdom is available to anyone who wants to come in."

The last thing Jesus said to Pilate was, *"Everyone on the side of truth listens to Me."* A more accurate rendering would be, "Everyone on the side of truth *hears* Me." This is a very important point because it has to do with "connecting" to Jesus' message. Everywhere I go teaching the message of the Kingdom, I find that it resonates with people from all religions and walks of life. God created us for kingship—for dominion—and inside each of us is a latent kingdom consciousness striving for expression. This consciousness reveals itself in various ways, such as in our natural resistance to being ruled or controlled by any other person and our continual longing to control the circumstances of our own lives. That is what finally connected me to Jesus—when I realized that He could teach me how to run life, not let life run me. I learned that I could control my own circumstances.

The search for power is a natural human drive. We all seek power over things and over circumstances, and that is what the Kingdom of Heaven promises. Jesus said, "I will testify to the truth of the Kingdom, and when you hear Me, you will believe it. You will connect with what I have to say because it will resonate with the kingdom consciousness that is already in you." We connect with the Kingdom message because it addresses the most deep-seated longing of our heart—our longing to be kings.

While it is natural to desire power over things and circumstances, desiring *power* over people is another matter. Seeking to *influence* people, public opinion, and public policy through kingdom principles is always appropriate, but pursuing despotic power *over* other people for personal gain at their expense is a corruption of our natural quest for power. Desiring to control our own life is one thing; desiring to control others' lives is another.

The King Is Central to His Kingdom

If we were created for kingship, and if Jesus came to earth to restore the kingship we lost, and if we want to be prepared to resume our rightful place as kings, then we had better learn what it means to be a king and how a king relates to his kingdom. This is important both for teaching us how to think, speak, and behave like rulers and for teaching us how to relate properly to God, our High King. A true king is not a dictator.

The first thing we need to understand is that *a king is the central component of his kingdom*. A king embodies the essence of his kingdom; the kingdom is the king. Without the king, there is no kingdom. The land and the people may still be there, but unless they are ruled by a king, they are not in a kingdom. This is one primary distinction between a kingdom and a democratic state. In a democracy, the country's leader, whether called a president or a prime minister or whatever, is *not* the center of the government. The constitution is. Presidents and prime ministers change every few years, but the constitution provides continuity of law and government. In a kingdom, the king is the constitution. His word *is* the law. His word *is* the government.

Second, *a king is the ultimate and only source of authority in his kingdom*. In the Kingdom of Heaven, the authority of God the King is exclusive and absolute. His word is law and His will is carried out even to the farthest reaches of His realm. And God's realm is infinite.

The sole and absolute authority of the King is what distinguishes the Kingdom of Heaven from religion. Religious people give lip service to God's kingship but then turn around and debate, question, and even amend His laws. For example, the King says that homosexual behavior is an abomination (see Lev. 18:22), yet a gathering of bishops who supposedly honor the King's law install an openly and actively homosexual priest as an archbishop! In the Kingdom, the King's word is *law*. It is not open to debate, discussion, challenge, or amendment.

While this may seem restrictive or even despotic to someone raised in a democratic environment, in many ways it actually relieves a lot of pressure. If you are under the King and someone asks you, "What do you think about so-and-so?" you can defer to the King's authority: "What I think does not matter. I am bound to follow my King, and my King says this…" or "I agree with my King, and this is what He says…"

In a democracy, political leaders campaign, negotiate, compromise, and consult committees in an effort to reach a consensus for establishing law and policy. In a kingdom, the king speaks…and that's it; no debate or question. The authority of the King is like the slogan that began circulating years ago: "God said it, I believe it, and that settles it." Even better is the variation: "God said it and that settles it, whether I believe it or not."

Jesus demonstrated this kingly authority when He said numerous times, *"You have heard…but **I** tell you…"* (see Matt. 5:21-22,27-28, 33-34,38-39,43-44, emphasis added). The biblical account of this occasion records:

*When Jesus had finished saying these things, the crowds were amazed at His teaching, because He taught as **one who had authority**, and not as their teachers of the law* (Matthew 7:28-29, emphasis added).

Jesus spoke and taught on His own authority. He did not rely on the thoughts, ideas, interpretations, or traditions of others. Why? Because He was a King whose authority was independent and sovereign.

This leads to a third point to understand about a king: *The sovereignty of a king is inherent in his royal authority.* The people do not make a king sovereign; he is born sovereign. Jesus told Pilate that He was *born* a king; He did not receive His kingship—or His sovereignty—from the hand of men. Sovereignty means freedom from external control. As sovereign, a king is free to do as he pleases with no accountability to anyone else in the kingdom. Otherwise, a king has no true authority. No one has the authority to tell God what to do. God's sovereignty is absolute. He is completely self-determining.

Fourteen Characteristics of a King

A king is distinct both from a democratically elected leader, such as a president or prime minister, as well as from a dictator in a totalitarian state. Following are 14 characteristics of a king that clarify that distinction.

1.   **A king is never voted into power.** His power is inherent from birth. Democratic leaders are *elected* to power; totalitarian dictators seize power; but a king is *born* into power.

2.   **A king is king by birthright.** His kingship is not conferred by men. Elected leaders rule by the will of the people. Dictators rule through fear, repression, and coercion. A king rules because he is born to it. Jesus Christ was born a King. We do not make Him King; all we can do is acknowledge that He *is* King.

3.   **A king cannot be voted out of power.** Because the
     kingdom is his by birth, a king rules for life. A presi-
     dent is voted out of office or departs due to term limits.
     A dictator may be brought down by a coup d'etat or
     popular uprising. Kingship, however, is a lifelong office.
     A human king may be dethroned by force or revolution,
     but he can never be voted out. The King of Heaven
     reigns by sovereign right of creation. He will never be
     voted out of power. Nor will He ever be dethroned.
     Lucifer tried and failed. Human empires have tried and
     failed and then fallen themselves, as is the destiny of all
     regimes that challenge His sovereignty. He was King
     before this world began, and He will still be King after
     it has passed away. In fact, Scripture makes this bold
     declaration:

*The kingdom of the world has become the kingdom of our Lord
and of His Christ, and He will reign for ever and ever* (Revelation
11:15b).

     No act either of man on earth or of the spiritual powers
     of darkness will ever remove the King of Heaven from
     His throne.

4.   **A king's authority is absolute.** That is why he is not
     a president or a prime minister. Presidents must con-
     sult Congress, and prime ministers, Parliament. If the
     prime minister of the Bahamas makes a decision, the
     senate can discuss it, the parliament may attack it, the
     media may mutilate it, and he may change his mind.
     Dictators, on the other hand, while perhaps exercis-
     ing absolute power (for a time), possess no *legitimate*
     authority. This is why they must use force and repres-
     sion to stay in power. But when a king speaks, he speaks
     with absolute authority—authority that is inherent to
     his kingship.

5. **A king's word is law.** Because a king's authority is absolute, his word is law. No one can countermand his orders, negate his pronouncements, set aside his decrees, or amend his statutes. David, an Israelite king who loved the King of Heaven with all his heart, had this to say about his King's law:

The law of the Lord is perfect, reviving the soul. The statutes of the Lord are trustworthy, making wise the simple. The precepts of the Lord are right, giving joy to the heart. The commands of the Lord are radiant, giving light to the eyes. The fear of the Lord is pure, enduring forever. The ordinances of the Lord are sure and altogether righteous....By them is Your servant warned; in keeping them there is great reward (Psalm 19:7-9,11).

The King's word is law. Great reward follows obedience. Disobedience brings severe penalties.

6. **A king personally owns everything in his domain.** Presidents and other elected leaders do not own their countries; they are citizens like everyone else. Dictators often act as though they own everything, but whatever they possess they acquire by fraud, theft, and corruption. A king, on the other hand, personally owns everything in his domain. In fact, a kingdom is the only form of government where the ruler owns everything and everyone. In the words of King David, once again:

The earth is the Lord's, and everything in it, the world, and all who live in it (Psalm 24:1).

The King of Heaven Himself declares:

Every animal of the forest is Mine, and the cattle on a thousand hills (Psalm 50:10).

A king owns the people, the animals, the plants, the land, and the air around the land. He owns the value under the earth—the gold, the silver, the platinum, the diamonds, etc. He owns the soil and the seeds in the soil. A king owns everything in his territory. That is why he is called a lord. Lord means owner. We'll discuss more on this concept in the next chapter.

7.   **A king's decree is unchanging.** In a democratic system, laws can be amended, revised, or revoked. Dictators change and even reverse their own decrees whenever it suits them. They renege on their word all the time. But a king's word is law. Once a king issues a decree, it cannot be changed.

Daniel, a faithful, God-fearing Jew in exile, was a high official in the court of Darius, a Medo-Persian king. When Daniel's enemies plotted to destroy him, they persuaded Darius to issue a decree that for 30 days no prayers or petitions were to be raised to any god or anyone else except to the king himself. Violators would be thrown into a den of lions. This decree was a "*law of the Medes and Persians, which may not be revoked*" (Dan. 6:8b NASB).

Catching Daniel in the act of praying to God in violation of the king's decree (as they knew they would), Daniel's enemies took him to the king. Darius was trapped. Even he could not revoke his own decree! The king spent a tormented, sleepless night while his trusted servant Daniel cooled his heels in the lion's den. The Lord delivered Daniel safely, and his enemies ended up with the lions instead.

The point here is that a king's decree, once issued, cannot be undone. The decrees of the King of Heaven are just as permanent:

The grass withers and the flowers fall, but the word of our God stands forever (Isaiah 40:8).

Jesus the King said:

Heaven and earth will pass away, but My words will never pass away (Matthew 24:35).

8.   **A king chooses who will be a citizen.** In a democracy, the citizens choose their leader while a totalitarian system treats its "citizens" as little more than tools of the state. A kingdom operates in the opposite manner—the king chooses the citizens. Because his authority is absolute, he determines the standards of citizenship in his kingdom. The people do not vote for the king, but in essence, he votes for them.

Jesus demonstrated this kingly prerogative as well when He said to His closest followers:

You did not choose Me, but I chose you and appointed you to go and bear fruit—fruit that will last. Then the Father will give you whatever you ask in My name. This is My command: Love each another. If the world hates you, keep in mind that it hated me first. If you belonged to the world, it would love you as its own. As it is, you do not belong to the world, but I have chosen you out of the world. That is why the world hates you (John 15:16-19).

Jesus chose them out of citizenship in the world and made them citizens of His Kingdom with full benefits of citizenship. They no longer belonged to the kingdom of the world. Now, like Jesus, their Kingdom was from another place. Jesus does the same thing today for everyone who believes Him—everyone who accepts His message of the Kingdom.

9.   **A king embodies the government of his kingdom.** This means that wherever a king is, his entire

government is present. Whenever a king speaks, his whole government is speaking. Whenever a king moves, the government moves with him because he embodies the government; the king is the government.

When President Bush travels abroad, the *authority* of the United States government travels with him because he represents the government and the people. The government itself, however, does not travel with him. It remains in place and functioning in Washington. The government of a king, on the other hand, is wherever the king is. A king and his government are inseparable. This is how we can know that the Kingdom of Heaven is on earth; the Kingdom is here because the King is here. Jesus said:

...if two of you on earth agree about anything you ask for, it will be done for you by My Father in heaven. For where two or three come together in My name, there am I with them (Matthew 18:19-20).

and:

...All authority in heaven and on earth has been given to Me. Therefore go and make disciples of all nations...teaching them to obey everything I have commanded you. And surely I am with you always, to the very end of the age (Matthew 28:18-20).

The Kingdom of Heaven is here because the King of heaven is here in the hearts and lives of His citizens who populate His colony here.

10. **A king's presence is the presence of his authority.** When a king shows up, his full authority is present. His authority does not reside in a place or in a document; it resides in him personally. This is why citizens of God's Kingdom colony on earth can act with kingly authority. Because the King is present, His authority is

present also. It was this present authority that Jesus had in mind when He said:

I tell you the truth, whatever you bind on earth will be bound in heaven, and whatever you loose on earth will be loosed in heaven (Matthew 18:18).

and:

I will do whatever you ask in My name, so that the Son may bring glory to the Father. You may ask Me for anything in My name, and I will do it (John 14:13-14).

Kingdom citizens may always exercise kingly authority because the King is always present with them.

11. **A king's wealth is measured by his property.** The larger and richer in resources a kingdom is, the wealthier the king, because the king owns everything in his kingdom. Dictators become wealthy by stealing from the people. Democratically elected leaders may or may not be personally wealthy, but they definitely do not own their country. This is one of the major distinctions between a king and other government leaders. Kings own everything in their domain by right of birth and kingship. As a matter of fact, property is so tied up with a king's identity that without it a king is not a king. We will discuss this more thoroughly in Chapter Six.

Why is wealth so important in a kingdom? So the king can take care of his citizens. A righteous and benevolent king does not amass wealth for himself but for the welfare of his citizens. This is why it is only in a kingdom where we truly find *commonwealth*; that is, the wealth is common to all the people.

No kingdom is greater or richer than the Kingdom of Heaven because it encompasses all that exists. And no king is wealthier than the King of Heaven because He owns everything everywhere in both the natural and supernatural realms. Consequently, no citizens of any government are more prosperous or have greater welfare than do citizens of the Kingdom of Heaven because all the infinite wealth of that Kingdom is their common wealth.

12. **A king's prosperity is measured by the status of his citizens.** If the citizens are poor, the king is seen as a poor king. If the citizens are prosperous, however, the king is seen as a wealthy king. Wealthy citizens make a king proud. That is why it is important for a king to make sure his people prosper. Jesus never preached prosperity. Why not? Because prosperity is a matter of Kingdom business. Anyone who becomes a citizen of the Kingdom of Heaven automatically prospers because the King of heaven is a wealthy King—the wealthiest of all. And He is also a righteous and benevolent King who is committed to the fullest and greatest welfare of His people.

13. **A king's name is the essence of his authority.** A king can delegate authority to anyone he pleases to act in his name or on his behalf. This is often done by issuing a "king's letter," a royal edict signed by the king and bearing his official seal that authorizes the bearer to act on his authority. Anyone to whom the king's letter is presented must treat the bearer as if he were the king himself.

Nehemiah, another exiled Jew who was a contemporary of Daniel, was cupbearer to the Persian king Artaxerxes. Hearing that Jerusalem had been destroyed, Nehemiah longed to go there and rebuild the city. When the king learned of Nehemiah's desire, he granted him permission to go. He also issued letters instructing the keeper of the king's forest to give Nehemiah all the material he required and for the governors of the various provinces to grant him safe passage. Nehemiah carried the king's name and, therefore, his authority (see Neh. chapters 1–2).

Citizens of the kingdom of Heaven have the same privilege. Jesus the King has issued king's letters to all His people, delegating His authority to them. That is why the New Testament says that Kingdom citizens are to pray in the name of Jesus. It is why He promised to do anything that they asked in His name. There is nothing religious or mysterious about this. It is simply a kingdom principle at work. The King's name carries the same authority as the King Himself, and all who carry His name can operate in His authority.

14. **A king's citizenry represents his glory.** Any conscientious king wants his citizens to be happy, prosperous, and content because their status and quality of life reflect on him. The greater their prosperity and well-being, the greater the glory and honor that rest on the king who provides for them so well. Citizens of God's Kingdom are supposed to show what their King is like by the way they live, act, dress, walk, and talk. Kingdom citizens are to reflect the nature and character of their King, who is righteous, just, benevolent, compassionate, and full of glory. This is why there is no poverty in the Kingdom of Heaven, no economic crisis, and no shortages. As King David observed:

The Lord upholds the righteous...I was young and now I am old, yet I have never seen the righteous forsaken or their children begging bread (Psalm 37:17b, 25).

The King of Heaven takes care of His citizens.

Appropriating the riches of the Kingdom of Heaven means first of all understanding that the King owns *everything* and we own nothing; and second, that He can give whatever He wants to anyone He wants whenever He wants. This is the kingdom concept of *lordship* and is the subject of the next chapter.

Principles

1. A kingdom is the sovereign rulership and governing influence of a king over his territory, impacting it with his will, his intent, and his purpose.

2. In the fullness of time, Jesus came to the earth and reestablished the Kingdom. Because only a king can establish a kingdom, this act alone reveals that Jesus Christ is the King.

3. Jesus said that His Kingdom was not *of* this world; He never said that it was not *in* this world.

4. Inside each of us is a latent kingdom consciousness striving for expression.

5. We all seek power over things and over circumstances, and that is what the Kingdom of Heaven promises.

6. A king is the central component of his kingdom.

7. A king is the ultimate and only source of authority in his kingdom.

8. The sovereignty of a king is inherent in his royal authority.

9. God's sovereignty is absolute. He is completely self-determining.

CHAPTER FIVE

Kingdom Concept #2:
Understanding the
Kingdom Concept of Lord

One of the most common words used in Scripture is the word *lord*. This word does not exist in democracies, socialist societies, or republics, except in the word *landlord*, in reference to one who owns land. Landlord is the only common remnant of kingdoms in modern governments and Western societies. Yet this concept of *lord* is one of the fundamental principles of a kingdom.

Every kingdom must have a king, but it is also true that every king is automatically a "lord." It is this quality of lordship that distinguishes a king from a president, a prime minister, a mayor, and a governor. As a matter of fact, a king's lordship makes him different from any other kind of human leader. Lordship makes a king unique.

In the last chapter we talked about a king's sovereignty—how a king is free from external control and he can do whatever he pleases with accountability to no one except himself. A king's sovereignty is absolute. He is neither voted into nor voted out of power; sovereignty is his by right of birth. The same is true of a king's lordship. All kings are automatically lords.

So what's the difference between a king and a lord? Lordship is only one aspect of a king's overall identity and status, but it is one of the most important ones. One way to put it is to say that *king* relates to *dominion*, while *lord* relates to *domain*. The word *dominion* refers to a king's authority—his power; the word *domain* refers to the territory, the property, the geographical area over which his authority extends. A king exercises authority (dominion) over a specific geographical area (domain) and within that area his authority is absolute.

Without a domain there is no king. A king is a king only so far as he has something to rule over. What good does it do to have authority if you have nowhere to exercise it? In that case, you really *don't* have authority. The most you have is *potential* authority. Until you have a physical domain over which to rule, your so-called "authority" is little more than theory.

If the word *lord* relates to a king's domain, then the lordship of a king is tied up in his territory. To put it another way, if kingship has to do with authority, then lordship has to do with *ownership*. Let me explain. If a king must have a domain in order to be a king, then *all true kings must have **and own** territory*. This is what we call the kingdom lordship principle. You cannot be a king unless you own property. It is not the same simply to exercise rule and authority over a geographical region. Presidents do that. Prime ministers do that. Governors do that. But presidents, prime ministers, and governors do not *own* the territory over which they rule, and therein lies the difference. Kings personally own the physical domain over which they reign, and that is what makes them not only kings but also lords. So king and property go together. And the word *lord* defines the king's identity as "owner" of his domain.

As lord, a king literally and legally owns everything in his domain: the forests and the meadows, the mountains and the valleys, the rivers and the streams, the crops and the livestock, even the people and the houses they live in. Everything in a king's domain belongs to him. Because of this, a king has absolute and unquestionable control over his domain. This goes back to a king's sovereign authority. A king is sovereign by right of birth, but he is also sovereign by right of ownership.

The fact of a king's sole ownership of his domain carries a couple of significant implications that are easily lost by people who have grown up in a democracy. First, and rather obvious, is that if the king owns everything, then no one in the kingdom owns anything. *In a true kingdom, there is no such thing as private property ownership. Kingdom citizens are stewards, not owners.* They may occupy the land; farm it; mine its minerals, ores, and precious gems; build houses and places of business on it; and carry on all the other normal activities of human communities; but they do all of these only by the king's permission and good pleasure. Ultimately, everything belongs to him.

Second, if the king owns everything, he can give anything to anyone at any time according to his own sovereign choice. In a democracy, if the prime minister or the president gives you property as a personal favor, it is called corruption. But if a king gives you property, it is called royal favor. And no one can question it or protest it because as owner, it is his prerogative to do as he pleases. Not only does a king possess the authority to distribute his property anytime, anywhere, to anyone, as much as he wishes, but he also can switch his property from one person to another. He can take something from one person and give it to you, or he can take something from you and give it to somebody else.

Because a king's dominion is so closely tied to territory, his wealth is measured by the size and richness of his domain. That is why kings always want to expand their kingdom; they seek to increase their wealth. Think about the British, French, and Spanish kingdoms of the last several hundred years. The kings of those realms dispatched ships and established colonies all over the world. Why? Because they wanted to enlarge the borders and fill the coffers of their kingdoms. The larger and richer their domain, the greater their reputation and glory.

King and Lord

Although I have been speaking about lordship from the context of earthly kingdoms, everything I have said so far applies with even greater validity to the Kingdom of Heaven and its King. We have already seen that God is the King of heaven and earth by divine right of creation; He is King of all because He created all. And because every king is automatically a lord, the King of all is also the Lord of all; He owns everything because He made everything.

The Bible, the constitution of the Kingdom of Heaven, plainly identifies God as King and Lord of all. One of the most common Hebrew words used to refer to God in the Old Testament is *adonai*, which literally means proprietor or owner. It is usually translated "lord." The personal name for God, Yahweh, although difficult to translate with complete accuracy, carries the same idea of master, owner, or lord.

This biblical picture of God as Lord is further enhanced by the fact that in most Bible versions, the personal name Yahweh, wherever it occurs, is replaced with the word "Lord." This is in keeping with an ancient Jewish tradition where devout Jews so respected and honored God's name that they would not even speak it or read it aloud to ensure that they did not inadvertently violate the Third Commandment by misusing His name. Instead, they substituted the word *adonai*, or "Lord."

So over and over the truth is hammered home: God is the Lord… God is the Lord…God is the Lord. This truth is reiterated even in the most basic confession of faith for a Jew, recited every morning:

Hear, O Israel: The Lord our God, the Lord is one. Love the Lord your God with all your heart and with all your soul and with all your strength (Deuteronomy 6:4-5).

So in this way the Jews were reminded every day that their God was Owner of all. This included Heaven and earth. An ancient Hebrew poet expressed it this way:

*May you be blessed by the Lord, the **Maker of heaven and earth**.
The highest heavens **belong to the Lord**, but the earth **He has
given** to man* (Psalm 115:15-16, emphasis added).

As Maker and Owner of heaven and earth, God could give any portion of it to anyone He chose. And He chose to give the earth to man,
not for man to be owner but ruler/manager, or steward. Here are some
additional references verifying God's rights to Lordship over the property
of earth:

*The earth is the Lord's, and everything in it, the world, and all
who live in it; for He founded it upon the seas and established it
upon the waters* (Psalm 24:1-2).

*For God is the King of all the earth; sing to Him a psalm of praise.
God reigns over the nations; God is seated on His holy throne. The
nobles of the nations assemble as the people of the God of Abraham, for the kings of the earth belong to God; He is greatly exalted*
(Psalm 47:7-9).

*And the Egyptians will know that I am the Lord when I stretch out
My hand against Egypt and bring the Israelites out of it* (Exodus
7:5).

O Lord, our Lord, how majestic is Your name in all the earth!
(Psalm 8:1a).

*I said to the Lord, "You are my Lord; apart from You I have no
good thing* (Psalm 16:2).

*The poor will eat and be satisfied; they who seek the Lord will
praise Him—may your hearts live forever! All the ends of the earth
will remember and turn to the Lord, and all the families of the
nations will bow down before Him, for dominion belongs to the
Lord and He rules over the nations* (Psalm 22:26-28).

The Lord is my shepherd, I shall not be in want (Psalm 23:1).

Lift up your heads, O you gates; be lifted up, you ancient doors, that the King of glory may come in. Who is this King of glory? The Lord strong and mighty, the Lord mighty in battle. Lift up your heads, O you gates; lift them up, you ancient doors, that the King of glory may come in. Who is He, this King of glory? The Lord Almighty—He is the King of glory (Psalm 24:7-10).

"The silver is Mine and the gold is Mine," declares the Lord Almighty (Haggai 2:8).

In the same way as the Old Testament reveals God as King and Lord and Owner of all, the New Testament reveals Jesus Christ as Lord and Owner of all. First of all, as we have already seen, Jesus came announcing the arrival and reestablishment of the Kingdom of heaven on earth, something only the King Himself could do. And because a king is automatically a lord, this means that Jesus is Lord also.

In addition, the most common Greek word for "lord," *kurios*, is applied to Jesus repeatedly in the New Testament. *Kurios* signifies having power. It also means one who possesses ultimate authority; master. Everything the Old Testament says about God as Lord, the New Testament says about Jesus.

The Lordship of Jesus is also by creative rights and was a natural result of His role in the creation of all things both seen and unseen. In essence, we do not "make" Jesus Lord; He is Lord by creative right, whether we acknowledge Him or not. In His preexistence before He came to earth, Jesus was identified as "the Word." It was in this dimension that He was the source of creation. Let us read the record of His creative activity that gives Him Lordship rights:

In the beginning God created the heavens and the earth (Genesis 1:1).

And God said, "Let there be light," and there was light (Genesis 1:3).

In the beginning was the Word, and the Word was with God, and the Word was God. He was with God in the beginning. Through Him all things were made; without Him nothing was made that has been made (John 1:1-3).

The Word became flesh and made His dwelling among us. We have seen His glory, the glory of the One and Only, who came from the Father, full of grace and truth (John 1:14).

But in these last days He has spoken to us by His Son, whom He appointed heir of all things, and through whom He made the universe. The Son is the radiance of God's glory and the exact representation of His being, sustaining all things by His powerful word (Hebrews 1:2-3a).

Here is ample evidence that Jesus as the eternal Word was responsible for the creation of the universe and for sustaining it.

One familiar story about Jesus drives this point home. Only a week before His death, Jesus was preparing to enter Jerusalem, but He intended to do it in a very specific way.

As they approached Jerusalem and came to Bethphage and Bethany at the Mount of Olives, Jesus sent two of His disciples, saying to them, "Go to the village ahead of you, and just as you enter it, you will find a colt tied there, which no one has ever ridden. Untie it and bring it here. If anyone asks you, 'Why are you doing this?' tell him, 'The Lord needs it and will send it back here shortly.'" They went and found a colt outside in the street, tied at a doorway. As they untied it, some people standing there asked, "What are you doing, untying that colt?" They answered as Jesus had told them to, and the people let them go (Mark 11:1-6).

In this story, Jesus acted in His authority as Lord. There is no indication that He had prearranged this with the owner of the colt or that He asked anyone's permission. As Lord of all, He owned the colt anyway. Jesus just told His disciples, "Bring me the colt." When challenged, all the disciples had to say was, "The Lord needs it." That was all it took; the owners released the colt.

In those days, animals such as that colt were valuable commodities as beasts of burden and as transportation. They were like a car is to us today. So untying that colt was no small matter. The modern day equivalent would be as if Jesus had said, "Go down to the corner, where you will find a brand-new silver Mercedes sport coupe. The keys are already in it. Bring it here to me." In the end, one word from the Owner of the colt was all that was necessary. The manager/steward of the colt let it go.

Another New Testament passage also presents Jesus clearly as Lord of all. It is found in a letter written by Paul, the Kingdom of Heaven's ambassador to the Gentiles, to Kingdom citizens in the city of Philippi:

> *Your attitude should be the same as that of Christ Jesus: who, being in very nature God, did not consider equality with God something to be grasped, but made Himself nothing, taking the very nature of a servant, being made in human likeness. And being found in appearance as a man, He humbled Himself and became obedient to death—even death on a cross! Therefore God exalted Him to the highest place and gave Him the name that is above every name, that at the name of Jesus every knee should bow, in heaven and on earth and under the earth, and every tongue confess that* **Jesus Christ is Lord**, *to the glory of God the Father* (Philippians 2:5-11).

Jesus Christ is King and Lord of all.

Living Under a Lord

It is the lordship aspect of a kingdom that makes living in a kingdom better than a republic or any other form of national administration or rulership. Lordship in a kingdom protects the citizenship from competition with their fellow citizens for national resources. It destroys such elements as jealousy, fear, deceit, and hoarding. In a true kingdom, the lord owns all resources and distributes the same as he determines.

Whenever he gives resources to a citizen, it is never for ownership but for stewardship. Submission to a king as lord positions the citizen to receive from the king.

From a kingdom standpoint, then, the most important confession any of us could ever make is to declare, "Jesus Christ is Lord." Ambassador Paul stated this explicitly in his letter to the believers in Rome when he wrote:

If you confess with your mouth, "Jesus is Lord," and believe in your heart that God raised Him from the dead, you will be saved (Romans 10:9).

By "saved," Paul means redeemed, bought back, salvaged, restored from the estrangement of our rebellion against God the King into a right relationship with Him. The key affirmation in that process is our acknowledgment that Jesus is Lord of everything, including our lives and our destiny.

But if we say, "Jesus is Lord," what does that mean in practical terms? What does it mean to live under a "lord"? The only experience most westerners have with a lord of any kind is with a landlord. If you now live or have ever lived in rental property, you know that the landlord is the landowner (or the landowner's direct representative who exercises the landowner's authority, which amounts to the same thing), the person you pay rent to and to whom you are accountable for the way you treat his property. Why? Because you do not own the property; the land*lord* does.

Dealing with a landlord provides a small taste of what it would be like to live all of your life under a lord. If you say, "Jesus is Lord," you are acknowledging His authority over you as well as your responsibility to obey Him. There is no such thing as lordship without obedience. If He is Lord, you cannot say, "Lord...but," or "Lord...except," or "Lord...wait." If He is Lord, the only thing you can say is, "Lord...yes."

Jesus Himself reiterated this truth throughout His public ministry:

If anyone would come after Me, he must deny himself and take up his cross daily and follow Me (Luke 9:23b).

Anyone who loves his father or mother more than Me is not worthy of Me; anyone who loves his son or daughter more than Me is not worthy of Me; and anyone who does not take his cross and follow Me is not worthy of Me (Matthew 10:37-38).

Another disciple said to him, "Lord, first let me go and bury my father." But Jesus told him, "Follow Me, and let the dead bury their own dead" (Matthew 8:21-22).

If Jesus is Lord, He must receive first priority in your life. He is above every other love and every other loyalty. He is above every goal, dream, and ambition. You cannot be a disciple and say, "Lord, *first* let me..." He must be first...in *everything*. Otherwise, He is not truly Lord of your life, regardless of what you say. Jesus said:

Why do you call me, "Lord, Lord," and do not do what I say? (Luke 6:46).

You cannot call Him Lord and then start making excuses for not obeying Him. You can't claim that He owns you and then go ahead and do whatever you please. In the Kingdom of Heaven there is no such thing as a "weekend citizen." You do not follow Him one time and not another depending on your preference. If Jesus is Lord, you cannot live for Him on Sunday and for yourself the rest of the week. Jesus is either Lord *of* all, or He is not Lord *at* all. The Lordship of Christ is a 24/7 proposition. There is no other schedule.

Living under a Lord also means giving up all concepts of personal ownership. This does not mean you have to sell your house or sell your car or give away all your personal possessions. It does mean learning not to take a proprietary view toward these things. The King of Heaven is a righteous and benevolent Lord who graciously allows us to use and fully appropriate His riches and resources and all good things. That is one of our rights as Kingdom citizens. We can enjoy all of these things without measure as long as we remember who owns them. The moment we begin to think that they *belong* to us, however, we set ourselves up for trouble. If we think ownership is ours, we make ourselves a lord. This takes us out of alignment with the will and character of the King because in His Kingdom there can be only one Lord.

What happens when we think of ourselves as owners? In our dog-eat-dog culture it means we feel we have to fight for what we get, hoard what we have, and guard it anxiously from fear that someone will take it away. And our neighbors do the same thing. We live in fear of economic downturns, inflation, downsizing, and never having enough. This is *not* Kingdom thinking!

In the Kingdom of Heaven, there is no economic crisis and there are no shortages. With a King who owns everything, how could there be? When we relinquish our sense of ownership and acknowledge God as the Owner and ourselves as stewards, it relieves us of the pressure of having to worry about how we are going to make it because we are now depending on Him for our welfare. And He is a benevolent and generous Lord of infinite resources.

Relinquishing ownership then also puts us into the position of full access to those resources. As we learn to give and receive and transfer at His will, He shares with us freely and abundantly. But a hoarding sense of personal ownership that shouts, "Mine!" cuts us off from those same resources. Which position would *you* rather be in?

Letting go of personal ownership also nourishes and releases a generous spirit within us. If we are only stewards and not owners, we can give freely as the Lord has given freely to us, knowing that He, who has no limitations, can replace what we give to others. His reputation as King and Lord rides on how well He cares for His citizens and He will give special care to those citizens who reflect His character by giving as He gives.

As a matter of fact, the best time to give is when things are tight personally because that is when you acknowledge that He owns even what you don't have. The greatest sign that you truly believe that Jesus is

Lord is by how much you are willing to get rid of. You have learned how to live under a Lord when you can give freely without hesitation, regret, or fear and say to the Lord of all with a joyful and willing spirit, "It's all Yours! It's all Yours!"

Seven Points in Summary

In summary, here are seven fundamental principles of lordship.

1. A king personally owns everything in his domain. There is no private ownership in a kingdom. Everything belongs to the king.

2. Use of anything in a kingdom is a privilege. If the king owns everything, then anything in that kingdom that we use is not by right but by a privilege granted by the king.

3. A king can give or distribute anything to anyone in his kingdom. Why? Because he owns it. He can shift things around any way he pleases. This is why we need to hold onto "our" possessions lightly. They really are not ours. Sometimes the King will test us by telling us to give up something He has given us. Our response— obedience or disobedience—will reveal whether or not we really believe He is Lord. If we obey, we show that we believe He owns everything and that He not only can replace what we give but even multiply it.

4. Submission to a king's lordship means that we have no right to ourselves. That is why the greatest confession we can ever make is the confession, "Jesus Christ is Lord." The moment we say those words, we are acknowledging that we have no more right to our own life; it now belongs to Christ. We have put ourselves willingly under His control and direction and are at His beck

and call. He can help Himself to our lives anytime He wants.

5.   Obedience is acknowledgement of lordship. When we obey the King, we are simply saying to Him, "You are Lord and my life is Yours. Your wish is my command."

6.   Thanksgiving is an acknowledgement of the King's Lordship. Daily thankfulness for food, water, clothing, shelter, and other daily needs reveals that we believe that the King owns all and is the source of all we have.

7.   The word "Lord" can never be used with the word "but." Those two words are impossible together. We cannot say, "I love You, Lord, *but...*" or else He is not Lord. We cannot claim Him as Lord and then make excuses for not obeying Him. The only appropriate word to go with "Lord" is "Yes!" Either He is Lord *of* all, or He is not Lord *at* all.

Principles

1. All kings are automatically lords.

2. Kingship has to do with authority; lordship has to do with ownership.

3. All true kings must have and own territory.

4. As lord, a king literally and legally owns everything in his domain.

5. If the king owns everything, then no one in the kingdom owns anything.

6. If the king owns everything, he can give anything to anyone at any time according to his own sovereign choice.

7. A king's wealth is measured by the size and richness of his domain.

8. God, the King of Heaven, is King and Lord of all.

9. Jesus Christ is King and Lord of all.

10. The most important confession any of us could ever make is to declare, "Jesus Christ is Lord."

11. There is no such thing as lordship without obedience.

12. If Jesus is Lord, He must receive first priority in your life.

13. Jesus is either Lord *of* all, or He is not Lord *at* all.

14. Living under a Lord also means giving up all concepts of personal ownership.

15. In the Kingdom of Heaven, there is no economic crisis and there are no shortages.

16. Relinquishing ownership puts us into the position of full access to all of Heaven's resources.

17. Letting go of personal ownership also nourishes and releases a generous spirit within us.

CHAPTER SIX

Kingdom Concept #3:
Understanding the
Kingdom Concept of Territory

The essence of a kingdom is property. Land or property is the validation of a king. Land or property defines a king or queen and gives him or her right to claim kingship. Remember that the first thing God created in the creation narrative was property…the earth. Earth was created before mankind was formed because it was necessary in order for man to be a legitimate ruler. Man was created to dominate, and it is impossible to dominate nothing.

Thus the mandate of God to Adam was to be king over a property. Every kingdom must have territory. The word *kingdom* derives from the phrase "king domain." *Domain* refers to the property, the territory over which a king exercises his dominion. A "kingdom," then, is a "king's territory." Without territory, a king is not a king because he has nothing to rule over. You cannot be "king" over nothing.

Let me give you an example from history. The "discovery" of the new world by Christopher Columbus in 1492 set off a wave of westward expansion over the next several centuries. The great maritime empires of Europe such as England, France, Holland, Spain, and Portugal all competed for new territory in the Western Hemisphere. It was, in fact, the Portuguese monarchs Ferdinand and Isabella who sponsored and financed Columbus' epic voyage.

Portugal focused most of its attention on South America and eventually claimed the area that now comprises the nation of Brazil. For many years Brazil was a colony and a possession of Portugal. That is why to this day Brazilians speak Portuguese. It is a legacy of their years under Portuguese influence and control.

The story goes that the son of the king of Portugal said to his father, "I want to be king."

"Well," the king replied, "you can't be."

"Why not?"

"I am the king of Portugal, and we are in Portugal. You can't be king because I am still alive. When I am dead, then you will be king."

"But I want to be king now," the prince said. "I don't want to wait that long."

So the king of Portugal shipped his son off to South America and made him king over the territory of Brazil. The son was sovereign in Brazil but ruled as a regent under his father, the king of the Portuguese empire, which included Brazil. Whenever the father visited his son in Brazil, the son became the prince again until his father left. Then the prince was again king. Whenever the son visited his father in Portugal, he again became the prince until he returned to his own domain. If the son wanted to rule as king, it was better for him to stay away from his father.

That's how kingdoms work. All kingdoms have territory, but there can be only one sovereign to rule over it. More than one does not mean divided rule; it means revolt.

This picture also illustrates the relationship between God, the King of Heaven, and man, His regent on earth. Because God is a King, and because a kingdom is a country ruled by a king and must therefore have territory, we can draw the conclusion that Heaven is a *place*. It is not some nebulous, mystical idea from the mind of man. Heaven is a real Kingdom with a real government. The fact that its primary realm encompasses the spiritual dimension of creation does not make it any less real.

But the realm of the Kingdom of Heaven also takes in the natural world. God designed it this way when He created the earth and then fashioned man in His own image to rule it for Him. The sequence of events here is very important. God envisioned man to be a king in his own right, but a king is not a king unless he has territory over which to rule. So God prepared the territory first—the earth—and then brought forth man. God placed man on the earth and told him, "I am giving you dominion over this physical domain. You have authority over every acre of land and sea and over every creature that inhabits the earth. Rule it freely as My legal representative."

God does not want to come here where we are personally, so that we can retain our authority as earthly kings. This is also why Jesus is not anxious for us to go to the invisible country of Heaven because when we do, we are reduced to princes and princesses. He prayed that we would not be taken out of the world but be kept in it but away from evil. The earth is man's key to dominion power and his only legal territory for rulership.

A careful review of the model prayer of our Lord Jesus reveals that it specifically identifies the location of the Father and King of Heaven: "*Our father who is in Heaven....*" His location is the key to our power and authority on earth. If He comes to earth, we lose our privileged position. Mankind was designed to serve as a corporate rulership of kings representing their Father, the King of Heaven, in the colony called earth.

Like the Portuguese prince in the story above, man was sovereign within the sphere of his own domain, but he acknowledged God's ultimate sovereignty over all by right of creation and ownership. That ideal arrangement was shattered, however, when man rebelled against God, abdicated his regency, and passed control of his realm to a demonic usurper, a fallen angel who had no right or authority to take it.

God's purpose is unchanging. He created man for rulership, and so immediately set into motion His plan to restore to man the Kingdom he had lost. The Bible lays out a detailed record of the historical outworking of God's plan. In the fullness of time, when everything was in place, Jesus Christ, the Son of God, was born into human flesh and appeared to men, saying, *"Repent* [change your mind], *for the kingdom of heaven is near* [or has arrived]" (Matt. 4:17b). The Son of God came to get the Kingdom back for man. He came as a human because earth is man's God-given domain, and only a human has the legal authority to rule it directly.

Seven Kingdom Principles of Territory

Territory is vital to a kingdom because without territory no kingdom can exist. This is why a king is always interested in expanding his territory. Why is territory so important? Why can there not be a kingdom without it? Here are seven reasons.

1. **No king can rule nothing.** A king is a ruler, which by definition requires a domain to rule over. No domain, no ruler; no ruler, no king. That is why God made the earth before He made man; man could not be a king until he had a domain. When God set out to establish His Kingdom, He began by creating territory: *"In the beginning God created the heavens and the earth"* (Gen. 1:1). First He created Heaven, His territory, and then He created earth, man's territory. That way man could be a king like his Creator.

2. **There is no kingdom without a domain.** Why is the territory of a king called his domain? Because he dominates it. A territory dominated by a king is called

his "king dominion," which is where we get the word "kingdom."

3. **The essence of a kingdom is the right, the power, and the authority of the king to exercise complete sovereignty over a domain.** In other words, a true kingdom is one where the king has the *right* to rule. Rights are very important because they are the basis for authority. God has the right to rule the universe. Why? Because He created it. Within His Kingdom God can do whatever He wants because His rights as King give Him absolute power and authority—infinite power and authority because His Kingdom is infinite.

4. **The heart of the kingdom concept is king domain.** The domain of the king is the key to his kingdom because to be a king he has to have some domain to rule.

5. **A king is not a king without a domain.** I've already said this, but it bears repeating because many people who have no kingdom concept have trouble understanding the connection between a king and his domain. When the Shah of Iran was ousted by Islamic fundamentalist revolutionaries in 1979, he fled to another country. Although he was still called the shah (the Iranian word for king), it was mainly a courtesy. In reality, he was no longer a king because he no longer had a domain. He was a king *in exile*. You cannot be a king without territory. This is why Christ had to come to earth to get our earthly kingdom back. We are supposed to be rulers, but without our territory we cannot fulfill our destiny.

6. **The wealth of a king's domain defines his value.** We touched on this in the last chapter. Territory is important to a king because the more territory he has, the richer he is. A king is only as wealthy as his domain. And as we will see later, territory—real estate—is

important because it is the only form of earthly wealth that never loses its value.

7. **The loss of a domain is the loss of a kingdom.** Again, the Shah of Iran is a good example. As soon as he lost his domain he was no longer a king except in name. Another prime example is Adam. When Adam, the king of the earth, rebelled against God, the High King of Heaven, he lost his kingdom and with it, his place as king.

The Bible says that Jesus Christ is the "second Adam" who came to restore what the first Adam lost. Because Jesus restored the Kingdom, all who are citizens of the Kingdom of heaven can now be kings and queens of the earthly realm again. What does this mean in practical terms? It means we can control our circumstances and our domain rather than they controlling us. The "good news of the Kingdom" that Jesus preached is not just that we can have our sins forgiven and become aligned rightly with God, although these are absolutely essential; the good news is also the fact that we can have our Kingdom back!

Five Principles of Man's Earthly Authority

Our destiny as human beings is wrapped up in land. God created us to be kings over the earthly realm, and He will not rest until we are fully restored to our rightful place. I want to share with you five principles that help explain the basis of our authority on earth as God intended it to be.

1. **The first thing God gave man was territory.** He did not give man a religion or rules to follow. He gave him land. Before man could be the king God created him to be, he had to have a king domain to rule over.

2. **The earth was created to give man kingship legitimacy.** God gave us the earth so that our kingship would be legal. He made Adam a king and He made Eve a queen equal to Adam in every way. The rulership of the earth belongs to both men and women. My wife

is my partner in rulership. She does not serve me. We dominate the earth together on behalf of our government of Heaven.

3. **The domain of earth is mankind's legal right, power, and authority of rulership.** When God said, "Let *them* have dominion," He transferred the legal rights to the earth to us. He did not say, "Let *us* have dominion," including Himself, because He already had His dominion in heaven. He said, "Let them have dominion over that territory called earth. I'm going to rule heaven; My kids are going to rule earth. I'm going to be King of heaven; they're going to be king of the earth. I'm going to be Sovereign of heaven; they're going to be sovereign of earth." The dominion of earth is our legal right. We have a right to be here and God gave us that right. So many believers look forward to going to heaven, but I look forward to coming back to rule the "new earth" that God will fashion when this earth passes away! (see Rev. 21:1). Heaven is fine, and it will be a glorious place, but ultimately it is not where we belong. In heaven we have no legal authority to rule; it is God's domain. We were made for the earth, and that is where our place of dominion will be in the life to come.

4. **"Let them" are the key words in the transfer of authority from God to man.** God delegated authority to us because He wants us to experience rulership. He wants us to know what it is like to be in charge.

5. **Man's kingship is by privilege, not by creative right.** God controls the domain because He created it. He rules it by creative rights. We rule it because of privilege. We are kings by delegation, not by creation. God gave us rulership but not ownership. But our rulership

"charter" includes a *sense* of ownership because He gave
us sovereignty within our earthly dominion.

Binding and Loosing

This transfer of ruling authority over the earth from God to man
has major implications for all of us regarding our daily circumstances
and our relationship to our society and culture. Therefore, it is important that we understand it. God has given us authority over the earth.
That means *we're in charge*. Whatever we say goes. This gives us a lot of
freedom to do what we please within our domain. But it also means that
we can't blame God for everything that goes wrong, yet that is exactly
what we do. "Why does God allow so much suffering in the world? Why
doesn't God do away with evil? Why does He allow sickness to continue?
Doesn't He care? Why doesn't God do something?"

Why doesn't God intervene? Because this is not His domain. He
will not intervene in the affairs of this earthly domain without the permission of those who hold dominion authority here. And who holds
dominion authority? Every human being on earth who is a citizen of the
Kingdom of Heaven. God is not to blame for human evil and suffering.
We brought these things on ourselves by our own selfishness and rebellious spirit. God wants to help but won't intervene unless invited to do
so by Kingdom citizens who know their dominion authority. Through
prayer we invite God to act in our domain.

This is what Jesus meant when He said:

*I tell you the truth, whatever you bind on earth will be bound in
heaven, and whatever you loose on earth will be loosed in heaven*
(Matthew 18:18).

Many believers have been taught that this verse deals with binding
and loosing demonic spirits. It has nothing to do with demons. Jesus is
using Kingdom language. To "bind" means to lock up or prohibit; to
"loose" means to unlock or permit. On earth we have dominion authority. Jesus is saying that what we prohibit on earth, heaven will prohibit,

and what we permit on earth, Heaven will permit. Consider the implications of this. Whatever we allow in society, Heaven will not stop, and whatever we disallow in society, Heaven will make sure it does not happen.

Do you understand how serious this is? The management of the earth is totally up to us. *We* are responsible for the evil, ills, and suffering in our world. These things are reflections of the nature and quality of our management. That is why God needs us to pray. He cannot interfere on earth unless we release Him to do so because He has given us sovereignty here. When we do, Heaven invades our territory on our behalf.

The King of Heaven has given us dominion authority here on earth, and He will not violate it without our permission.

This truth holds a critical key to how we should live as Kingdom citizens on earth. Having been raised in one or another of the various human systems of government, we all have been "programmed" to think of life and society in terms of the "have's" and the "have not's," of periodic economic upheavals and downturns, chronic shortages of commodities, corruption, despotism, and the strong preying on the weak. We look at these things, sigh, and then say, "Oh well, that's life."

Not in the Kingdom of Heaven!

As I said before, in the Kingdom of heaven, there is no economic crisis and there are no shortages because heaven's resources are infinite. And because all Kingdom citizens are equal, there are no "have's" and "have not's"; everyone is a "have." There is no corruption or despotism because our King is a righteous and benevolent ruler. The strong do not prey on the weak because there are no weak. Everyone is strong in the strength and presence and influence of the King and in the secure knowledge of their place and privilege as equal citizens of the Kingdom.

Seeing life from this perspective will require a major change of mind-set for most people. We have to learn, we have to train, we have to be taught to think this way. A change of mind is what the Bible calls "repentance." So now the words of Jesus become much clearer when He says, *"Repent, for the kingdom of heaven is near"* (Matt. 4:17). He is saying, "Change your mind! Stop thinking like the world with its inadequacies and inequities, and start thinking like a Kingdom citizen! Stop operating from a worldly mind-set of "never enough" and start operating from a Kingdom mind-set of "more than enough"! The Kingdom of Heaven is here and everything has changed!"

Ten Principles of the Power of Land

I hope that by now it is becoming clear how important territory is to the kingdom concept. With this in mind, I want to conclude this chapter with a brief discussion of ten principles of the power of land. In this context, *land*, *territory*, and *domain* mean the same thing.

1. **The first thing God gave man was land.** We have already discussed this. God created the earth and then created man to rule it. Specifically, God placed Adam in a lush, beautiful garden and gave him the responsibility of caring for it and all its inhabitants. The King of Heaven gave the king of earth a physical domain—land—over which to exercise dominion.

2. **The first thing man lost was land.** When Adam and Eve rebelled against the king, He drove them out of the garden. They lost the property God had given them. Having lost their dominion, they discovered that the earthly environment was now hostile to them.

3. **The first thing God promised Abraham was land, not heaven. The first thing God promised Moses was land, not heaven.** Our big dream is to go to Heaven, while God's big dream is for us to possess land because He created us to be kings, and all kings own property.

4. **Real wealth is in the land.** That's why it's called real estate. All other estates aren't "real." So many people expend all their resources acquiring "wealth" that never

lasts—commodities that dissipate through consumption or are wiped out by economic depression or natural disaster. Land never loses its value regardless of what the economy does. In fact, land almost always grows in value even during difficult times. If you want to help ensure prosperity for yourself as well as future generations, focus on acquiring real estate. There is power in land, which leads us to the next principle.

5. **He who owns the land controls the wealth.** Once, I was in Omaha, Nebraska, riding in from the airport, and remarked to my driver about the beauty and impressiveness of a particular skyscraper that dominated the skyline. "What is that?" I asked. He chuckled and said, "That's the disgrace of the city." "Why?" I asked, surprised. He replied, "That's the tallest building in the city, and it is owned by the Japanese." Smart people—Kingdom-minded people—go after land. Why?

6. **True wealth is in the land.** It never loses its value and, in fact, almost always increases in value the longer you own it. I once acquired a small piece of land for $35,000. Several people made offers to buy the land, but I held on to it. A few years later, a wealthy businessman built a $3,000,000 estate on an adjacent piece of property. What do you think that did to the value of *my* land? True wealth lies in real estate.

7. **The meek will inherit the earth.** And Jesus said that is a blessing: *"Blessed are the meek, for they will inherit the earth"* (Matt. 5:5). "Meek" means "gentle," but it also means "disciplined." The Greek word refers to the demeanor of a horse that has been broken for riding. A horse is a very strong animal. After it is broken it is still strong, but that strength is now under control. It is under discipline. These kind of

people—the meek—Jesus says, are the ones who will inherit the *earth*—not Heaven.

8. **Land is the only estate that is real.** Real estate is the only property of truly lasting value that we can pass on to our children. Everything else fades away too easily. The Bible says: *"A good man leaves an inheritance for his children's children"* (Prov. 13:22a).

9. **God considers the loss of land a curse.** This is very important in the Bible. Every time God cursed the Israelites for their rebellion and disobedience, He took land from them. When they repented, He blessed them by restoring their land. God uses land to measure blessing or cursing. Therefore...

10. **The restoration of land is a blessing.** Land is important. Land has power because without land there is no domain and without domain there is no king.

Kings of a New Earth

Many Kingdom citizens have been taught so thoroughly to anticipate and look forward to Heaven as the ultimate "reward" for the life to come that talk of an earthly inheritance makes them uncomfortable. But this is what the Bible says. Isaiah, an ancient and early spokesman for the Kingdom of Heaven, recorded:

> *For this is what the Lord says—He who created the heavens, He is God; He who fashioned and made the earth, He founded it; He did not create it to be empty, but formed it to be inhabited—He says: "I am the Lord, and there is no other"* (Isaiah 45:18).

God created the earth for people to live on it. He is so committed to this planet that even when it passes away He will re-create it:

> *Then I saw a new heaven and a new earth, for the first heaven and the first earth had passed away....And I heard a loud voice from*

the throne saying, "Now the dwelling of God is with men, and He will live with them. They will be His people, and God Himself will be with them and be their God...for the old order of things has passed away." He who was seated on the throne said, "I am making everything new!" (Revelation 21:1, 3, 4b-5a).

God's program never changes. He is committed to His plan for earth, and for earth dwellers, which is why we can't stay in Heaven. The Bible promises a full resurrection in which all Kingdom citizens will have a new body, a physical body of some sort, and will reign in the earth forever, just as God intended from the beginning. In the meantime, He wants us to practice—to learn how to take up rulership and exercise wise dominion over this territory called earth that He has given us. The Kingdom of Heaven is here now. We are its citizens, representatives of its colonial government, and we possess the authority right now to act in the name of our King and bring the influence of His will and desires over this earthly domain.

Principles

1. Every kingdom has territory.

2. Heaven is a real Kingdom with a real government.

3. A king is not a king unless he has territory over which to rule.

4. The Son of God came to get the Kingdom back for man.

5. Without territory no kingdom can exist.

6. A king is only as wealthy as his domain.

7. Our destiny as human beings is wrapped up in land.

8. We were made for the earth, and that is where our place of dominion will be in the life to come.

9. We are kings by delegation, not by creation.

10. God will not intervene in the affairs of this earthly domain without the permission of those who hold dominion authority here.

11. Through prayer we invite God to act in our domain.

12. In the Kingdom of Heaven there are no "have's" and "have not's"; everyone is a "have."

13. The meek will inherit the earth, not Heaven.

CHAPTER SEVEN

Kingdom Concept #4:
Understanding the
Kingdom Concept of Constitution

After the invasion of Iraq by the military forces of the United States and the other alliance nations, the first objective after toppling Saddam Hussein was to create a new nation. It is interesting to note that the first order of business was to construct a constitution, and it took months for that exercise to be completed. The process of nation-building could not proceed until that document called the constitution was completed and accepted by all the principals involved.

The heart of all nations, empires, and kingdoms is the constitution. There is no nation or kingdom without a constitution. In a republic, the constitution is the covenant the people make with themselves and which they hire by vote, a governing body to keep that covenant for them and with them. In a kingdom, the constitution is the king's covenant with his citizens and his kingdom. In the case of the former, the constitution is produced by the aspirations of the people, while in the latter case the constitution is initiated by the king and contains the aspirations and desires of the king for his citizens and his kingdom. This is the primary

127

distinction between a kingdom and a democratic republic. For example, the Constitution of the United States begins with the words, "We the people...." However, when reading the constitution of the Kingdom of God as documented in the Scriptures, it always says, "I, the Lord, say..."

Like every other governmental system, every kingdom has a constitution. The constitution of any nation has to do with the manner in which the government of that nation is organized, particularly with regard to the way sovereign power is exercised. It embodies the basic laws and principles that guide that government and lays out the specific powers and duties of that government in relation both to the people and to other nations and governments. A constitution also delineates, guarantees, and protects the specific rights of the people who live under its jurisdiction.

Regardless of the type of government, a constitution is established by whoever exercises power. In a totalitarian state or a dictatorship, the supreme leader, along with a ruling elite of cronies appointed by him, determine the laws and conditions under which the people live—laws usually designed for their own benefit and enrichment at the people's expense.

In a republic or democracy, on the other hand, power lies with the people. They elect leaders to represent them and then petition those leaders to enact laws and policies that will benefit the electorate. In a democracy the leaders are answerable to the people. Those who fail to perform adequately or who violate the people's trust can be voted out and replaced. Through their elected leaders, the people establish their own constitution.

As noted earlier, a kingdom is different. In a kingdom all power resides in the king. It is the king, therefore, who establishes the constitution for his kingdom. The constitution of a kingdom is the documented will, purposes, and intent of the king. It expresses the king's personal desires for his kingdom and sets out the principles under which the kingdom will operate as well as establishing the manner and conditions of how the king will relate to his people and they to him. A kingdom constitution is stamped with the essence of the nature, character, and personality of the king. This is why it is always good to have a king who is righteous, benevolent, and compassionate, with a genuine concern for the welfare of his citizens.

A Royal Contract

In a kingdom, the constitution is a *royal contract* that the king has with his subjects—his citizens. It is *not* the contract that the citizens have with the king, and this is a very important distinction. In the first, the contract originates with the king and in the second, with the people. A contract generated by the people is a *democracy*, the complete opposite of a kingdom. A royal contract, on the other hand, originates completely and exclusively in the heart, mind, and will of the king. His citizens have no input concerning the terms or conditions of the contract.

This is the approach the King of Heaven has always taken with mankind. When God began to establish a Kingdom colony on earth, He set out all the conditions and parameters beforehand. Everything was already in place by the time Adam arrived on the scene. All Adam had to do was follow the terms and conditions that God had already established:

> *Then God said, "Let Us make man in Our image, in Our likeness, and let them rule over the fish of the sea and the birds of the air, over the livestock, over all the earth, and over all the creatures that move along the ground." So God created man in His own image, in the image of God He created him; male and female He created them. God blessed them and said to them, "Be fruitful and increase in number; fill the earth and subdue it. Rule over the fish of the sea and the birds of the air and over every living creature that moves on the ground"* (Genesis 1:26-28).

> *Now the Lord God had planted a garden in the east, in Eden, and there He put the man He had formed....The Lord God took the man and put him in the Garden of Eden to work it and take care of it. And the Lord God commanded the man, "You are free to eat from any tree in the garden; but you must not eat from the tree*

of the knowledge of good and evil, for when you eat of it you will surely die (Genesis 2:8,15-17).

As you can see, this entire contractual process was completely unilateral on God's part. Adam had no input at all; in fact, when the contract was drawn up, he wasn't even around yet! After he was created, Adam simply received the completed contract from the hand of the King.

The same is true regarding God's contract with Abraham. First, God determined what He was going to do and then presented Abraham with the completed contract:

The Lord had said to Abram, "Leave your country, your people and your father's household and go to the land I will show you. I will make you into a great nation and I will bless you; I will make your name great , and you will be a blessing. I will bless those who bless you and whoever curses you I will curse; and all peoples on earth will be blessed through you" (Genesis 12:1-3).

After this, the word of the Lord came to Abram in a vision: "Do not be afraid, Abram. I am your shield, your very great reward."…He took him outside and said, "Look up at the heavens and count the stars—if indeed you can count them." Then He said to him, "So shall your offspring be" (Genesis 15:1,5).

Such unilateralism on God's part is an expression of His sovereignty. To both Adam and Abraham (Abram) God was saying, "This is *My* government; this is the agreement I am making with *you*. You don't dictate the terms or tell Me what you want. I tell you what I want for you and what I will do for you." A kingdom constitution is initiated *by* the king, *from* the king, and for the king's pleasure.

A kingdom constitution, then, is the document that constitutes the king's desire for his citizens. In a republic, the constitution is the people's contract with themselves, while in a kingdom it is the king's contract for the people. In a democracy, the people plan and decide what they want to happen to them. But in a kingdom, the people have no say. Instead, the king tells you what he wants to happen to you.

This is why God would make a statement like:

For I know the plans I have for you…plans to prosper you and not to harm you, plans to give you hope and a future. Then you will call upon Me and come and pray to Me , and I will listen to you. You will seek Me and find Me when you seek Me with all your heart. I will be found by you… (Jeremiah 29:11-14).

So the Kingdom constitution states the King's desires for His citizens. And because He is a righteous and benevolent King, His desires are always for our greatest good and benefit. The King of heaven wants to bless us; He wants blessings to overtake us. We are always trying to tell God what to do, especially today: "Here's what I want, here's what I want, here's what I want…." But God says, "In *this* Kingdom, *I* make the contracts."

The King's Will and Testament

In addition to being a royal contract, the *constitution* in a kingdom constitutes the expressed will of the king. It is the king's will *expressed* in tangible, written form. This means that the constitution is not limited to an oral contract. Putting the constitution in written form sets it up as a standard that can be measured easily as well as making its terms and conditions clear to everyone. This is why in the Kingdom of Heaven we have a *book* called the Bible. The Bible is the expressed will of the King in written form. It is the constitution of His Kingdom.

As we have already seen, the words of the king become the law of the land. His words do not produce the contract; his words *are* the contract. And out of this contract—this constitution—comes the law. The constitution is not the law; the constitution produces the law. What I mean is that the constitution establishes the terms, conditions, and rights of life in the kingdom. This leads to laws designed with the express purpose of ensuring that all of those terms, conditions, and rights are preserved, protected, and accomplished.

The constitution is the will and the testament of the king for his citizens. *Will* and *testament* are two different but related words that are both important. A *will* is what is in the mind of a person—his or her desire and intent. A *testament* is the physical documentation of a person's will, codifying his or her desire and intent in the form of a legal document. A will, then, is in your head; a testament is when you write down what is in your head. This is why lawyers always ask, "Do you have a will *and* testament?" The written testament clarifies to all parties your desire and intent and makes them verifiable in a courtroom.

That is why I call the Bible the *constitution* of the Kingdom of heaven. It is even divided into two sections called the Old *Testament* and the New *Testament*. The Bible, then, comprises God's *documented* thoughts concerning His citizens—His *expressed* will, desire, and intent for the human race He created in His own image. A will kept in one's head can never be defended in court. It is for this reason that God commanded Moses and all the other prophets in the Bible to *write*. He wanted a testament that could be *tested* or *contested* in the court of the universe. So we take the Bible and we bring it before the court of the universe and say, "This is what my King guaranteed me." Then the King says, "According to My word, be it done unto you."

A testament provides protection from the abuse of rights. It protects the rights of the beneficiaries of the will. If all you have is a will, how can anyone know what you want for your beneficiaries? *You* know what you want, but what if you die suddenly? How will your beneficiaries be protected and receive the benefits you desire for them unless your will is written down and documented legally? That is the purpose of a testament. A testament can be contested in a courtroom. There is no doubt as to what you meant.

The Word of God, written down and printed in the book we call the Bible, is the most powerful document we have. It is the constitution of the Kingdom of Heaven, the testament of the will of the King for His citizens.

Seven Principles of the Kingdom Constitution

1. **The source of the constitution is the king, not the citizens.** Whereas the Constitution of the United States begins with the words, "We the people..." the constitution of God's Kingdom says, "I, the Lord..." We who live in democratic states can always amend our constitution because we, the people, created it. But we cannot change God's constitution because we didn't write it.

That is why I believe the biggest conflict in the coming years will be between the Kingdom and religion. Religious people keep trying to adjust God's constitution. They debate it and discuss it and become embarrassed or angry over parts they don't like. Sometimes they even change it or water it down to make it more palatable for modern spiritual tastes. This is absolute foolishness. The King of Heaven established the constitution for His Kingdom and only He can change it. But He won't. He is eternally unchanging, and so is His Word, because the King and His Word are the same. It says so right in the constitution:

The Lord is King for ever and ever; the nations will perish from His land (Psalm 10:16).

But the plans of the Lord stand firm forever, the purposes of His heart through all generations (Psalm 33:11).

Your throne, O God, will last for ever and ever; a scepter of justice will be the scepter of Your kingdom (Psalm 45:6).

But You, O Lord, sit enthroned forever; Your renown endures through all generations (Psalm 102:12).

Your word, O Lord, is eternal; it stands firm in the heavens (Psalm 119:89).

Long ago I learned from Your statutes that You established them to last forever (Psalm 119:152).

The Word of the King is unchanging and unchangeable. Yet hardly a day goes by without some religious leader somewhere going on some talk show or on a cable news channel and expounding his or her "opinion" about issues of the day that the Bible addresses plainly. When asked about gay rights or gay marriage or abortion or the like, they speak as if these and other matters are open to debate. In religion, perhaps, they are. *But not in the Kingdom of Heaven.*

In my travels all over the world, I am asked frequently to respond to these kinds of questions. I always frame my answer from a Kingdom perspective. A typical interchange might go something like this:

"Dr. Munroe, what do you think about homosexuality? What are your thoughts regarding abortion?"

"I have no thoughts about those things."

"But...you are supposed to be a man of God."

"I have no thoughts about these things because an ambassador never gives his personal opinion; it's illegal. My personal opinion is out of bounds. Others who represent a religion may express their opinions. But I do not represent a religion—not even Christianity. I represent a government—the Kingdom of Heaven. I am an ambassador, and ambassadors do not give their opinion. However, my government's position is..." and then I quote from the constitution—the Bible.

In the Kingdom of Heaven, we do not have the privilege of tampering with the constitution. It is not our document; it is the King's. And Kingdom citizens obey the law of the King.

2. **The constitution contains the benefits and privileges of the citizens.** It spells out the advantages that come with being a Kingdom citizen as well as everything the citizens can expect from the King. In the Bible, these often take the form of promises. Here are just a few:

Do not worry, saying, "What shall we eat?" or "What shall we drink?" or "What shall we wear?" For the pagans run after all these things, and your heavenly Father knows that you need them. But seek first His kingdom and His righteousness, and all these things will be given to you as well (Matthew 6:31-33).

Ask, and it will be given to you; seek and you will find; knock and the door will be opened to you. For everyone who asks receives; he who seeks finds; and to him who knocks, the door will be opened (Matthew 7:7-8).

For God so loved the world that He gave His one and only Son, that whoever believes in Him shall not perish but have eternal life (John 3:16).

I tell you the truth, whoever hears my word and believes Him who sent me has eternal life and will not be condemned; he has crossed over from death to life (John 5:24).

Do not let your hearts be troubled. Trust in God; trust also in Me. In My Father's house are many rooms; if it were not so, I would have told you. I am going there to prepare a place for you. And if I go and prepare a place for you, I will come back and take you to be with Me that you also may be where I am (John 14:1-3).

Again, I tell you that if two of you on earth agree about anything you ask for, it will be done for you by My Father in heaven. For where two or three come together in My name, there am I with them (Matthew 18:19-20).

Do not be afraid, little flock, for your Father has been pleased to give you the kingdom (Luke 12:32).

Each of these benefits, or promises, was spoken by Jesus, the Son of God who came to earth in human flesh to announce the return and restoration of the Kingdom of Heaven on earth.

3. **The king obligates himself to the tenets of the constitution.** A king and his word are the same, and when he speaks, his word becomes the constitution. So when a king's word is spoken (or written down), the king is

obligated to carry it out. That is why the Bible states that whatever God says, He will do and whatever He promises, He will bring to pass. Once the King of heaven speaks, it is as good as done. God cannot fail to keep His Word, for if He did, He would cease to be God.

4. **The constitution contains the rights established by the king for the citizens.** In addition to the benefits and privileges accruing to Kingdom citizens, the constitution also delineates and sets forth their rights. Rights in a constitution are important because they are the grounds for making law, which is the next stage. If I said to you, "I give you my car, my house, and my boat," I have just expressed my will. If I then document it on paper, it becomes a testament and your constitution. Now I have to make sure that laws exist to protect what I gave you. At that point, I would call in a lawyer to draw up a formal document because a lawyer knows the law of the environment to protect the piece of paper that states my will for you. The lawyer reads it and makes sure it is in a certain form where it becomes integrated into the system of society with the rights to protect it.

Then, if someone contests it, you can go to court. The court is the law, and the court says, "This is a legal document. Everything written here he has a right to receive." So the constitution contains your rights, and the laws protect them. Therefore, the constitution is the *source* of law; it is not the law itself.

If God says, "I will bless you, I will prosper you, I will make your name great…" that's constitution. If He then says, "…if you obey Me and keep My word, and walk uprightly," He has given you laws that set the conditions for the benefits and privileges to apply. The government says you are free to do commerce, to lease, to buy property, etc., as long as you pay taxes, do not break the law, obey the social order, and respect people's property. They give you all these constitutional rights, but they are contingent upon your honoring the laws. The Kingdom of Heaven is no different.

5. **The constitution cannot be changed by the citizens—only by the king.** This principle should be perfectly clear by now and needs no further elaboration.

6. **The constitution is the reference for life in the kingdom.** How are Kingdom citizens supposed to live? What are the values, the ethics, the moral code, and standards of behavior for citizens of the Kingdom, and where can they be found? In the constitution. God's standards for life in His Kingdom are found throughout the Bible. Such standards as these:

You shall have no other gods before Me. You shall not make for yourself an idol. You shall not misuse the name of the Lord your God....Remember the Sabbath day by keeping it holy....Honor your father and your mother....You shall not murder. You shall not commit adultery. You shall not steal. You shall not give false testimony against your neighbor. You shall not covet... (Exodus 20:3-17).

And:

Blessed are the poor in spirit, for theirs is the kingdom of heaven. Blessed are those who mourn, for they will be comforted. Blessed are the meek, for they will inherit the earth. Blessed are those who hunger and thirst for righteousness, for they will be filled. Blessed are the merciful, for they will be shown mercy. Blessed are the pure in heart, for they will see God. Blessed are the peacemakers, for they will be called sons of God. Blessed are those who are persecuted because of righteousness, for theirs is the kingdom of heaven (Matthew 5:3-10).

7. **The constitution contains the statutes of the kingdom.** Statutes are fixed, predictable standards. "Teach me Your statutes," King David of Israel says. Normally,

where the word "statutes" shows up, you will find "laws" in the same sentence. Statutes give the physical image of law. That's why we call a carving in stone a statue. Or we call it an image. Image is the same as statue. A statue is permanent. A statue means simply a fixed, predictable image or standard. Think about a statue in your town. When it rains does the statue change? What if it snows? What if the temperature tops 100 degrees? If you spit on it, curse it, hate it, does the statue change? Of course not. It remains the same no matter what.

A statute is the same way. That is why laws are called statutes. A statute does not adjust itself to the times. A statute does not accommodate the environment. It remains consistent within the changing environment. A statute is not affected by the conditions around it. Some people think the constitution of the Kingdom of Heaven needs to be changed or "reinterpreted" to accommodate modern times, values, and mores. On the contrary, the Kingdom constitution is an unchanging standard against which all modern values, mores, beliefs, and ideas must be measured. Without some dependable, righteous, unchanging standard, society will collapse. We can see signs of it all around us.

The constitution contains the statutes of the Kingdom. One time Jesus said these words: *"Heaven and earth will pass away before My statutes change. I will move the heavens and the earth before I move My statutes"* (see Luke 16:17; 21:33). Who are we to dare to think that we have the right or the authority to change or set aside the statutes that the King of Heaven has set in place? Religious people can do that any time they want, because they are not really in the Kingdom. Kingdom citizens, however, cannot. Our constitution says, *"The word of the Lord stands forever"* (1 Pet 1:25a).

Principles

1. Every kingdom has a constitution.

2. The constitution of a kingdom is the documented will, purposes, and intent of the king.

3. In a kingdom, the constitution is a *royal contract* that the king has with his subjects—his citizens.

4. A kingdom constitution is the document that constitutes the king's desire for his citizens.

5. The constitution in a kingdom *constitutes* the expressed will of the king.

6. The Bible is the expressed will of the King in written form. It is the constitution of His Kingdom.

7. The words of the king become the law of the land.

8. The constitution is the will and the testament of the king for his citizens.

9. The Bible comprises God's *documented* thoughts concerning His citizens—His expressed will, desire, and intent for the human race He created in His own image.

CHAPTER EIGHT

Kingdom Concept #5: Understanding the Kingdom Concept of Law

In any civil society, the "rule of law" is the bedrock of order and social justice. As noted in the previous chapter, a constitution is the documented aspirations, desires, and hopes of the people for themselves (in the case of a democratic republic), and in a kingdom, the king's aspirations and desires for his citizens. Law is produced to protect the constitution and to secure the rights of the citizens to what the constitution promises and guarantees them.

No human society can survive long without laws. This is just as true for a kingdom as for any other system of government. Human nature being what it is, laws are necessary to keep man's baser instincts and drives in check, protect public safety and decency, and preserve the moral order. Every kingdom is governed by laws. Laws enforce and protect the standards by which the kingdom operates.

As we saw in the previous chapter, the standards of operation for any government, a kingdom included, are codified in a document called the constitution. This contract spells out what the government expects from the people and what the people can expect from the government. It also delineates the rights of the people. These rights and expectations need to be protected, and that is the purpose of laws. A country's laws always reflect its constitution because they are derived from its tenets. They not only protect the standards and ensure their fulfillment, but also prescribe penalties for any who violate the standards.

In order to develop a better understanding of the overall kingdom concept, it is important to have knowledge of the origin, nature, and function of laws in a kingdom. And as I have throughout this book, I will continue to use the Kingdom of Heaven as the primary model. The Bible, the Kingdom of Heaven's constitution, establishes the standards for life in the Kingdom. Unlike other constitutions, however, it also lays out the penalties for noncompliance. In addition to being a constitution, then, the Bible is also the law book of the Kingdom of Heaven.

We often think of laws as unpleasant and inconvenient demands that restrict our freedom and limit our options. In reality, laws are designed to free us to pursue unlimited options by providing a safe environment where we can live in peace, security, and confidence. True freedom is always circumscribed by boundaries, and laws define those boundaries. Within those boundaries we are free to thrive, prosper, and reach our full potential.

For example, looking again at a passage we examined in a different context in Chapter Three, consider some of the positive benefits we derive from the laws of the King:

The law of the Lord is perfect, reviving the soul. The statutes of the Lord are trustworthy, making wise the simple. The precepts of the Lord are right, giving joy to the heart. The commands of the Lord are radiant, giving light to the eyes. The fear of the Lord is pure, enduring forever. The ordinances of the Lord are sure and altogether righteous. They are more precious than gold, than much pure gold; they are sweeter than honey, than honey from the comb.

By them is your servant warned; in keeping them there is great reward (Psalm 19:7-11).

What does the "law of the Lord" do for us? It revives our spirit, gives us wisdom, and fills us with joy. It enlightens our minds and emboldens us with confidence because of its permanence and uprightness. It enriches us with wealth much greater than earthly riches and leaves a sweet taste in our mouths. It warns us against danger and foolishness that could destroy our lives and places us on the path to "great reward."

If we allow it, the "law of the Lord" will nourish us thoroughly body, soul, and spirit. Jesus said:

It is written: "Man does not live on bread alone, but on every word that comes from the mouth of God" (Matthew 4:4).

This means there is more to life than food. We need solid, dependable, unchanging standards to live by; standards founded on truth. Many people today question or out-and-out reject the idea of absolute truth. Well, regardless of what they think, the Bible is absolutely true, and everything in it will work for our good if we obey it. There is no law in the Bible that is not good for humanity's overall welfare. In fact, the Bible is the best regulator of civic society, yet most of global society rejects its wisdom and insists on choosing its own path. That goes a long way in explaining the mess our world is in today. We need to take a closer look at the kingdom concept of law.

Seven Principles of Law

1. **All creation was designed to function by inherent principles.** *Inherent* means "built-in"; existent from the beginning. In other words, the laws of the King of Heaven are built into the very structure of creation and determine precisely how all of creation functions. Scientists speak of the laws of nature, the laws of physics, the laws of gravitation, the laws of thermodynamics, and many other laws to explain how nature works. In

this sense, laws are observable, measurable, and repeatable because they never change. Everything that God created was designed to function by certain built-in or inherent principles.

2. **These principles are called "natural law."** Natural law has to do with laws concerning the nature of a thing. For example, birds do not have to be taught to fly; that ability is inherent in them as a natural law. In the same way, fish are not taught to swim; they possess swimming ability as an inherent law. The same principle applies to plants when they produce seeds that reproduce new plants that are just like the original.

3. **Natural law is the standard for effective function of everything that God has created.** If birds follow the law of nature, they live and reproduce. If plants follow the laws of nature, they grow and produce fruit. God built these laws into nature, and as long as plants and animals follow those laws, they prosper and flourish. Violation of natural law, on the other hand, leads to dysfunction. Take a fish out of water and it will malfunction. It will die because a fish is designed to live and breathe in the water, not out of it. So natural law is very important; it is the standard for determining effective function.

4. **Laws are the key to successful existence and a guarantee of fulfillment of purpose.** Obedience to laws promotes prosperity and ensures success. All a bird has to do to fulfill its purpose is fly and reproduce; both of these functions are governed by natural laws. Every plant and creature on earth will succeed and fulfill its purpose simply by obeying the natural law inherent within them. It is no different with us. As long as we acknowledge the laws of God and submit ourselves willingly to living by and obeying them, we too will

succeed and fulfill our purpose in God's design. We will realize our full potential.

5. **Laws protect purpose.** When we obey laws, we protect the purpose for which we were born. As long as a fish stays in water, it will be able to survive and prosper. As long as a seed stays in the soil, it will sprout, grow, and prosper. As long as a bird stays in the air and there is space to fly, it will fulfill its purpose and prosper. As long as we obey the laws of God, we too will live and grow and prosper.

Please understand that when I talk about obeying God's laws in order to live and prosper, I am not suggesting that we can "earn" right standing with God by doing good works or by strictly observing some code of rules or statutes. The only way to be rightly aligned with God is by changing our mind and turning away from our rebellion against Him (which the Bible calls "repentance"), placing our trust in Jesus' death to remove the guilt of our rebellion (giving up our self-reliance), and acknowledging Him as Lord (Owner) of our lives. By obeying God's laws, I mean living in willing submission to Him as King and Lord and honoring His Word as the unchanging standard of reference for our lives.

So then, what laws of God are we to obey? All of them, of course, and there are many. But here are the two most important:

Love the Lord your God with all your heart and with all your soul and with all your strength (Deuteronomy 6:5).

Love your neighbor as yourself (Leviticus 19:18b).

Jesus Himself identified these as the two most important commandments in the law of God. Kingdom ambassador Paul, in context with a discussion about the responsibility of Kingdom citizens toward civic earthly authority, commented on this second verse, saying:

Love does no harm to its neighbor. Therefore love is the fulfillment of the law (Romans 13:10).

Obey the law and it protects you. Disobey the law and you risk sacrificing your purpose.

6. **The purpose for law is to protect the constitutional covenant.** Laws exist to make sure that the provisions of the constitution are carried out consistently, equitably, and without prejudice for all citizens. For example, the constitution guarantees every citizen the right not to be convicted of a crime until proven guilty. Trial by jury is a law designed to protect that constitutional right for every citizen. In the Kingdom of Heaven, the laws of God are designed to protect and ensure the fulfillment of all terms of the covenant that God has with His creation. Typically, cutting a covenant involved the swearing of an oath of fidelity between the parties entering into the covenant. Because God's covenant with man is unilateral (meaning that we enter freely into a covenant He has already established), He alone can swear faithfulness. And the Bible says that this, indeed, is what He has done:

When God made His promise to Abraham, since there was no one greater for Him to swear by, He swore by Himself, saying, "I will surely bless you and give you many descendants." And so after waiting patiently, Abraham received what was promised....Because God wanted to make the unchanging nature of His purpose very clear to the heirs of what was promised, He confirmed it with an oath (Hebrews 6:13-15,17).

The constitutional covenant of the Kingdom of Heaven is backed up by the laws of God, which are the expressions of His unshakeable and unchanging Word.

7. **Laws are the conditions of covenant.** They are the terms under which, if followed, the covenant will operate. Virtually everything we buy these days comes with a covenant of laws and conditions called a "warranty." The manufacturer guarantees that if the product is used in accordance with the specified terms and conditions

of operation or function, it will perform as designed. If those terms and conditions are violated, the warranty "covenant" is nullified, and if the product then malfunctions, the manufacturer is free of responsibility.

It is no different in the Kingdom of Heaven. The King's covenant with us specifies blessings and benefits for compliance as well as consequences and penalties for noncompliance. As long as we observe the conditions of the covenant, all the blessings and benefits of the covenant are operative in our lives. If we violate the covenant, the "blessings clause" shuts down and the "consequences clause" kicks in.

The King's Words of Law

As I said before, laws are built into the very fabric of creation. Everything in the natural realm operates according to inherent principles. The same is true of the spiritual realm. The Kingdom of Heaven is like any other government in the sense that it has laws to protect it and assure that it operates according to God's intent. Laws establish God's Kingdom. And these laws were put in place long before the first human being arrived. And yet so often, we have the arrogance and the presumption to question God or challenge Him about His laws and the way He runs things.

The biblical character Job tried this, and it earned him a stern rebuke from the King. Afflicted by boils, grieving over the untimely deaths of all his children, and criticized mercilessly by his best "friends," who urged him to confess his sins to God, Job held out, demanding to put his case before God Himself. Job knew he was innocent of any wrongdoing and could not understand why he was suffering. In his pain and indignation, Job ended up trying to tell God a few things. That is when God spoke up and adjusted Job's thinking:

Then the Lord answered Job out of the storm. He said: "Who is this that darkens My counsel without knowledge? Brace yourself like a man; I will question you, and you shall answer Me. Where were you when I laid the earth's foundation? Tell Me, if you understand. Who marked off its dimensions? Surely you know!...Do you know the laws of the heavens? Can you set up God's dominion over the earth? (Job 38:1-5a,33).

In other words, God was saying, "Job, how dare you ask Me about My laws? You weren't even around when I made them! Who are you to challenge Me?" It does no good for a product to challenge the manufacturer: "Why did you make things thus and so?" That is the manufacturer's prerogative. When you buy a car with an internal combustion engine, you have to accept the "law" that it requires gasoline to operate. It was the manufacturer's decision, not yours. No matter how hard you might try or how much you wish it otherwise, that car will not run on any other kind of fuel. That's why it is foolish to challenge God and useless to try to change His laws. God's laws were here long before we were, and they will still be here long after we are gone.

Laws are built into creation. And laws always carry consequences for violation. If you try to defy the law of gravity by stepping out of a second-story window, you are in for a painful shock—*if* you survive the fall! When we violate the law, we receive the due penalty. God doesn't have to judge us; the law carries its own built-in "judgment."

Remember, the king's word is law in his kingdom. When it is written down, it is called a testament, and when repeated verbally, constitutes a commandment:

When Moses went and told the people all the Lord's words and laws, they responded with one voice, "Everything the Lord has said we will do." Moses then wrote down everything the Lord had said (Exodus 24:3-4).

The "words and laws" Moses spoke to the people were the Ten Commandments and related laws that are recorded in the preceding chapters of Exodus. Like all of God's laws, the Ten Commandments are not religious dictates. They are laws established by the King of creation to determine how all the natural realm should function and how human beings should relate to God and to each other.

The Meaning of Law

What exactly is "law"? The most basic Hebrew word for "law" is *torah*, which also means, in addition to "law," direction and instruction. In time, the word *torah* was used to refer to the entire body of law that Moses received from God on Mt. Sinai and passed along to the Israelites. In this usage, torah means "the law," "the direction," and even "the Law of the Lord."1 In the New Testament we find two basic Greek words used for "law." The first of these is *nomos*, which means "to divide out, distribute" and also "that which is assigned." It gradually came to mean "usage" and "custom" and, eventually, "law as prescribed by custom, or by statute."2 This is the word from which we get our English word *norm*.

Whatever becomes accepted as a *norm* **in** our society eventually becomes a *law* **of** our society. If we are exposed to a certain unaccustomed idea or behavior long enough, we eventually become so used to it that we start to accept it. Once we accept it, we begin to think of it as "normal," or as a "norm." And once we see it as a norm, we start to *expect* it. Once we come to expect it, it becomes in practical terms no different from a law, even if it is never formally established as a legal statute.

Depending on the nature of the idea or behavior, this process could be very dangerous because we as a society could end up endorsing and normalizing evil or immorality. This is precisely what has happened and is happening in western culture with regard to such issues as homosexual rights, homosexual marriage, abortion rights, assisted suicide, embryonic stem cell research, and the like.

God's laws are designed to prevent us from accepting and normalizing evil and assigning it the force of law in our society. This is the protective nature of laws. They prevent ideas and behaviors that are contrary to the constitution and the good of the state and the people from becoming a dominant influence. In other words, God's laws are designed to protect the whole community.

This is why sin and violation of the law never affect only the person or persons directly involved, but many others as well. It is like a ripple effect. Our actions, good or bad, affect those around us in ways we may never know. When the Israelites were attacking the city of Ai during their conquest of the land of Canaan, the sin of *one man*, Achan, led to the defeat of the entire community. Only after the Israelite community dealt with Achan's sin were they able to achieve victory (see Joshua chapters 7–8). God's laws have *personal* application with *national* ramifications.

Another meaning of *nomos* is that of a decreed law established by a state. This definition applies perfectly to the Kingdom of Heaven because that Kingdom is a state; it is a country. For citizens of the Kingdom of Heaven, the Bible is the *nomos*, the decreed established law of the Kingdom that we are pledged and obligated to obey. It is a mistake to think of the Bible as a religious book. It is not. The Bible is a legal book, a book of laws that God has established and set forth in written form to define and protect His Kingdom as well as to protect, preserve, and deliver the entire community of mankind.

The second Greek word for "law" in the New Testament is *ethos*, which means "custom." Whenever we speak of something as being "customary," we are speaking of *ethos*. God's laws are supposed to be customary for us. It is supposed to be customary for us not to lie or steal or covet. It is supposed to be customary for us to forgive and to love our enemies as well as each other. *Ethos* is less formal than *nomos*. In fact, whereas *nomos* came to mean decreed, established law, *ethos* was used to describe *unwritten* law. The most powerful laws of all are the unwritten laws. In any culture, customs generally carry the social force of law even without formal legal establishment. And customs quite often have a greater influence on people's behavior than any formal laws that are on the books.

God never intended to write down any of His laws for us. He did not want us to have to read in order to live. There was no written law in the garden of Eden, no written law for Abraham, no written law at all for God's covenant people until the days of Moses. The King of Heaven's intention was to write His laws on our hearts and in our minds so that no one would have to teach us. It was humanity's rebellion and separation from God that made written law necessary. We needed something to restrain our baser nature and instincts and prevent us from destroying ourselves by uncontrolled selfishness, passion, and violence.

The King's goal has never changed. Despite mankind's rebellion, His original purpose still stands:

> *"This is the covenant I will make with the house of Israel after that time," declares the Lord. I will put My law in their minds and write it on their hearts. I will be their God, and they will be My people"* (Jeremiah 31:33).

This unchanging purpose of the King was fulfilled in the new covenant through Jesus Christ.

Natural Law versus Written Law

God intended law to be natural. To understand the Kingdom of Heaven, it is important also to understand the distinction between natural law and written law.

First of all, written law is necessary only when natural law is absent. If we human beings were all law-abiding by nature, there would be no need for written law. But as we saw above, our rebellion against God destroyed the rule of natural law in our lives and made written law (as well as human government) necessary to protect society and restrain evil.

Second, the purpose for written law is to restore natural law to the conscience. Because of our rebellion against God, we lost our instinctive knowledge and understanding of natural law. Our consciences became corrupt and our likeness to our Maker became tarnished and distorted. Things that were natural in the beginning now became "unnatural." For example, we consider generosity to be a virtue, a positive quality we admire in others and aspire to in ourselves. Why? Because it is *not* a "natural" human trait, at least not anymore. God never commanded Adam to be generous and giving. Why not? Because giving came naturally to Adam. A generous spirit was inherent in him because he was made in the image of God, his Creator, and God is generous by nature. But after the rebellion, mankind became greedy, obnoxious, abusive, mean, stingy, and hoarding. We needed a law to restore to our conscience the concept of giving.

Third, natural law is sometimes referred to as the "spirit of the law." This reflects God's desire for His laws, the standards of His Kingdom, to become the norms of our society. Remember, earth is a colony of Heaven, and the laws of the King of heaven should apply here as much as they do there. Laws produce society because they determine social relationships.

There is a difference between the law and the spirit of the law. The spirit of the law refers to original intent—the purpose that was in the mind of the Lawmaker in the beginning. Therefore, the spirit of the law is the inherent essence of the original purpose and intent of that law. As such, the spirit of the law is always higher and broader than the letter of the law. For this reason, the greatest form of law is unwritten law. Unwritten law is a product of the spirit of the law. When law has to be written, it is because the people are disobedient. Written law is a sign that the people have lost sight of the spirit of the law—the original intent. So where the spirit of the law is, there is no need for written law.

Any nation is only as good as the laws it enacts. Laws produce society, so whatever kind of society we want is determined by the laws we make. The worse the laws, the worse the nation. However, bad laws do not cause a nation's social, moral, and spiritual decline. They merely reflect a decline that is already underway. Laws mirror the condition of the nation.

This is why it is so important for we who are Kingdom citizens to regain our understanding of the "spirit of the law"—natural law. Natural law is the fundamental operating principle of the Kingdom of Heaven.

The laws of the King protect and preserve not only His Kingdom but also the benefits and privileges of the Kingdom that are reserved for Kingdom citizens. But learning to appropriate them involves more than just knowing what they are. We must learn also the *keys* of the Kingdom that unlock our benefits and privileges and make them active in our lives.

Principles

1. Every kingdom is governed by laws.

2. The Bible is the law book of the Kingdom of Heaven.

3. The Kingdom of heaven has laws to protect it and assure that it operates according to God's intent.

4. Laws are built into creation.

5. Whatever becomes accepted as a *norm* **in** our society eventually becomes a *law* **of** our society.

6. God's laws are designed to prevent us from accepting and normalizing evil and assigning it the force of law in our society.

7. God's laws have *personal* application with *national* ramifications.

8. Written law is necessary only when natural law is absent.

9. The purpose for written law is to restore natural law to the conscience.

10. Natural law is sometimes referred to as the "spirit of the law."

11. Laws produce society because they determine social relationships.

12. The spirit of the law is the inherent essence of the original purpose and intent of that law.

13. Any nation is only as good as the laws it enacts.

14. Natural law is the fundamental operating principle of the Kingdom of Heaven.

Endnotes

1. W.E. Vine, Merrill F. Unger and William White, Jr., *Vine's Complete Expository Dictionary of Old and New Testament Words* (Nashville, TN: Thomas Nelson Publishers, 1996), Old Testament section, 133-34.

2. Vine, Unger and White, *Vine's Complete Expository Dictionary*, New Testament section, 354.

CHAPTER NINE

Kingdom Concept #6:
Understanding the
Kingdom Concept of Keys

Every nation and social civil society functions on laws and customs that make that society work. These functions depend on the
constitution and a body law that create a context and reference
for social behavior and relating to the government and other members
of the society. The result is a culture of laws and principles that serve as
regulations, values, morals, and standards that govern the citizen's relationship with the authority structure and its disposition as it relates to
expectations within the constitutional framework. In essence, all nations
and kingdoms contain inherent principles and laws that must be adhered
to by each citizen in order for the citizen to benefit from his citizenship
privileges and rights. These laws and principles are called by Jesus, "Keys
of the Kingdom."

Have you ever found some old keys lying around your house and
couldn't remember what they were for? Possessing a key you cannot identify or match to a particular lock is as bad as not having a key at all. What
good are keys you can't use? They are as useless as locks you can't open.

This is exactly the problem with many believers today. We have a big bunch of "keys" called "Scriptures" that most of us don't know how to use. We have the keys, but we don't know which key unlocks which lock. It's like having all of this information but not knowing how to use it, having all of this power available to us but not knowing how to apply it.

Knowledge of the Word of God is important, but insufficient by itself for effective living as a believer. This is because most believers lack a proper Kingdom mind-set. Life in the Kingdom is really about returning to the governing authority of God in the earth and learning how to live and function in that authority. Part of understanding the Kingdom is learning how to use the keys of the Kingdom.

The Kingdom of Heaven is God's desire and purpose for us. Jesus said:

Do not be afraid, little flock, for your Father has been pleased to give you the kingdom (Luke 12:32).

Our Father, the King of heaven, has given us the Kingdom. It is ours. In fact, Jesus Himself brought the Kingdom to us. It was His main purpose in coming to earth in human flesh. We receive the Kingdom through His death. The moment we turn from our rebellion against God and place our trust in Christ to salvage us from the consequences of that rebellion, we become naturalized citizens of the Kingdom of heaven, with all the rights, benefits, and privileges that come with it. But how do we appropriate our rights? How do we enter into the full enjoyment of our benefits and privileges? What are the keys to effective living in the Kingdom?

Keys of the Kingdom

One day Jesus asked His disciples, His inner circle of 12 most intimate followers, the most important question He would ever ask them.

When Jesus came to the region of Caesarea Philippi, He asked His disciples, "Who do people say the Son of Man is?" They replied,

"Some say John the Baptist; others say Elijah; and still others, Jeremiah or one of the prophets." "But what about you?" He asked. "Who do you say I am?" Simon Peter answered, "You are the Christ, the Son of the living God." Jesus replied, "Blessed are you, Simon son of Jonah, for this was not revealed to you by man, but by My Father in heaven. And I tell you that you are Peter, and on this rock I will build My church, and the gates of Hades will not overcome it. I will give you the keys of the kingdom of heaven; whatever you bind on earth will be bound in heaven, and whatever you loose on earth will be loosed in heaven" (Matthew 16:13-19).

In the Jewish faith of that day, the titles "Christ" and "Son of the living God" were reserved exclusively for the Messiah, the deliverer of Israel and hope of the world who had been prophesied for centuries. So Simon Peter here was confessing his belief that Jesus was the Messiah. Jesus tells Peter that he did not arrive at this knowledge through his own understanding; it was given to him through supernatural revelation.

Then Jesus says that upon the "rock" of Peter's confession of faith, He will build His "church." The Greek word for "church" is *ecclesia*, a word that is widely misunderstood. Because it is translated here as "church," most people believe that *ecclesia* is a religious word. It is not. *Ecclesia* is a governmental term. It literally means "called-out ones" and was used by the Greeks to refer to the senate or other political groups that were chosen by the "democrat," or government. The Greeks invented the concept of democracy but never really applied it. But when the Romans overran the Greek empire, they adopted much of Greek thought and philosophy, including democracy, and developed them. This is how Caesar developed such a powerful government.

In the Roman Empire, the senate—the *ecclesia*—was like the cabinet in a modern democracy. The senate was the powerhouse. These individuals were handpicked by the emperor to receive his thoughts, his desires, his passion, and his intent. Their job was to take the mind of the king and turn it into legislation that could be implemented in the kingdom.

In other words, they were to know his mind and see that everything he wished was carried out. This meant that they had to stay in close contact with him. They had to talk to him, and he had to give them information about what he wanted in the kingdom.

The fact that Jesus used *ecclesia* to describe the body of followers that He was establishing tells us two things. First, the word *church* itself is a political rather than a religious term. And second, this entire discussion about keys and about binding and loosing is not a religious but a political discussion.

In effect, Jesus was saying, "In the same way that Caesar is lord of his government, and has created his senate, his *ecclesia*, his cabinet, I also will build My cabinet on the fact that I am the Christ, the "anointed king," the Lord of lords and Son of the living God." He said to Peter, "Upon the 'rock' of your confession of who I am, I will build My *government*. I will build My senate, My cabinet, My administrators who will carry out My wishes and My will." So Jesus established not a religion but a political force.

The *ecclesia*, therefore, is a secret group entrusted with secret information critical for the operation of the Kingdom. This group will be so powerful that even the "gates of hades will not overcome it." Another way to translate that phrase is, "the gates of hades will *not prove stronger than* it." Even hell itself will not be as strong as the ecclesia that Jesus is establishing.

What is this "secret information" that Jesus gives His cabinet? He says, "I will give you the keys of the kingdom of heaven; whatever you bind on earth will be bound in heaven, and whatever you loose on earth will be loosed in heaven." He gives them—gives us—the keys *of* the Kingdom, not the keys *to* the Kingdom. As Kingdom citizens, we are already in the Kingdom; we don't need the keys to it. What we need—and what Jesus has given us—are the keys of the Kingdom—the keys that will unlock the power of the Kingdom and make it work in our lives. Kingdom citizens and *only* Kingdom citizens have these keys. Citizenship in the Kingdom is a prerequisite for getting them.

What this means is that we who are Kingdom citizens are supposed to be operating on a level that blows other people's minds. We should have access to a power that mystifies those who are not yet in the Kingdom. We are supposed to be living life at a certain level where we are tapping into resources that others cannot explain.

Knowledge of the Secrets

The key to keys is not *having* keys. The key to keys is *knowledge*, knowing what the keys are for and how to use them. On another occasion Jesus told His "cabinet":

> *The knowledge of the secrets of the kingdom of God has been given to you* (Luke 8:10a).

The Kingdom of heaven is not a secret society, but its keys have to be learned. A secret is anything you don't know, especially if somebody else does. Miracles fall into this category. A miracle is something that humans cannot explain, an event or occurrence that seems to defy the laws of nature. These men had seen Jesus walk on water, heal the sick, raise the dead, shrivel a tree by speaking to it, calm a storm, multiply bread, and many other "miraculous" things that were beyond the ken of human experience.

But to Jesus, none of these were miracles. He said, "These are no miracles; I'm just using keys. I know how to put them in the locks, and they are unlocking prosperity, unlocking healing, unlocking peace, unlocking authority. Watch Me and you will see the Kingdom at work, and also how it should work for you. My Father has given you the knowledge of the secrets of the Kingdom. I will teach you how to use the keys."

Jesus left no doubt that the Kingdom was supposed to work for His *ecclesia* just as it worked for Him, for on the night before His death He told them:

> *I tell you the truth, anyone who has faith in Me will do what I have been doing. He will do even greater things than these, because I am going to the Father. And I will do whatever you ask in My*

name, so that the Son may bring glory to the Father. You may ask Me for anything in My name, and I will do it (John 14:12-14).

Jesus' ecclesia (which includes us) was going to do the same things He was doing—and more—because the Holy Spirit who would come after He was gone would teach them the keys of the Kingdom and how to use them. One significant key is embedded in this passage: the key to opening the "warehouse" of Heaven. The key that opens that lock is *prayer*—asking in *Jesus' name*—and *whatever* and *anything* we ask will be done. That is a wide-open promise, but it is not a way to gratify our own selfish wants and desires. We must use the right key. We must ask in Jesus' name—according to His will and in line with His purpose. That is what will open Heaven's floodgates.

The twelve disciples of Jesus had already seen this key activated in unforgettable fashion the day Jesus fed five thousand people with fives loaves of bread and two fish. The crowd had been with Jesus all day listening to His teaching. Now it was late in the day, and they were hungry. Jesus' disciples suggested He send them away into the villages to get food, but Jesus has another idea. He was preparing to teach them how to use a key:

> *Jesus replied, "They do not need to go away. You give them something to eat." "We have here only five loaves of bread and two fish," they answered. "Bring them here to Me," He said. And He directed the people to sit down on the grass. Taking the five loaves and the two fish and **looking up to heaven, He gave thanks** and broke the loaves. Then He gave them to the disciples, and the disciples gave them to the people. They all ate and were satisfied, and the disciples picked up twelve basketfuls of broken pieces that were left over. The number of those who ate was about five thousand men, besides women and children* (Matthew 14:16-21 emphasis added).

Jesus used this situation to test His disciples to see if they picked up on the secrets. He said, "You feed them." That was the test. They should have asked, "Which key do we use?" Instead, they said, "All we have is…." They were limited by what they could *see*. But in the Kingdom of Heaven we walk not by sight but by faith. The lesson Jesus wanted them (and us) to learn is that when you know the keys to the Kingdom secrets, you will never again say, "All I have is…."

Look at the progression: Jesus looked up toward heaven and gave thanks. He put in the key of prayer and unlocked the warehouse. Then He broke the bread, gave it to His disciples, and they distributed it among the people. It should work for us the same way. Through prayer *in Jesus' name* (the key), we unlock Heaven's warehouse. The King Himself draws forth from its abundance and gives it to us, and we then give it to others.

But we have to know the key that opens the warehouse. That knowledge is Christ's promise to us: *"The knowledge of the secrets of the kingdom of God has been given to you."*

Seven Principles of Keys

Knowledge leads to understanding. Once we know the principles behind keys, we can understand how they work in the Kingdom. There are several principles that define the properties of keys.

1. **Keys represent authority.** If you possess a key to a place, it means you have authority in that place. Suppose your boss entrusts you with a key to the store or the office. By doing so, he shows not only that he trusts you but also that he has delegated a certain amount of authority to you. The key to your house means you have authority there. The key to your car gives you authority to drive whenever you want to. Christ says, "I am giving you the keys of the Kingdom of Heaven. I am giving you authority in heaven, the same authority I have." What an awesome gift! Few of us have done more than just scratch the surface in learning what this means.

2. **Keys represent access.** A key gives you instant access to everything that key opens. The secret is in knowing

what the key opens. The keys of the Kingdom of Heaven give us immediate access to all the resources of heaven. But we have to know how to use them. So often we limit ourselves by trusting or believing only in what we can see with our eyes or reason out with our minds. A Kingdom mind-set completely changes our perspective.

When a pagan king sent his army to capture the Hebrew prophet Elisha, the prophet's servant was terrified one morning to find the army surrounding the city.

> *"Oh, my lord, what shall we do?" the servant asked. "Don't be afraid," the prophet answered. "Those who are with us are more than those who are with them." And Elisha prayed, "O Lord, open his eyes so he may see." Then the Lord opened the servant's eyes, and he looked and saw the hills full of horses and chariots of fire all around Elisha. As the enemy came down toward him, Elisha prayed to the Lord, "Strike these people with blindness." So he struck them with blindness, as Elisha had asked* (2 Kings 6:15b-18).

Elisha's servant was frightened by what he *saw* around him, but he didn't have a key. Elisha had a key, unlocked heaven, and brought down an angelic host to protect them. The prophet tapped into a principle that took him to a system that made that pagan army look like toy soldiers by comparison. When you have the keys of the Kingdom, you have no lack and no crisis because the King is greater than them all. Jesus said He would teach us to walk in that kind of authority, access, and confidence.

3. **Keys represent ownership.** Possession of a key gives you de facto ownership of whatever that key opens. Therefore, when you possess the keys of the Kingdom of heaven, you have ownership of heaven on earth. Jesus said, *"Whatever you bind on earth will be bound in heaven, and whatever you loose on earth will be loosed in heaven."* In other words, you own on earth whatever is going

on in Heaven. This means that you should never judge how your life is going simply by your circumstances.

Suppose you get laid off from your job. It would be easy to get scared and stressed out because you have a family and bills to pay and no money. That's your circumstances. As a Kingdom citizen with the keys of the Kingdom, however, you have ownership of heaven on earth. You can be confident and even rejoice in the prospect of a bright future because you have a source of supply and provision that those outside the Kingdom cannot even conceive. So go have a prosperity party! The King is preparing to bless and prosper you from a completely unexpected direction. When you "own" the resources of the King, you are never destitute.

4. **Keys represent control.** If you possess the key to something, you control it. You control when it opens, when it closes, and who gets access to it. A key helps you control time. In other words, you decide whether to open it up at 8:00 or 10:00 or 6:00 or whenever. This gives you control over when something comes. If you need something now, you operate a key.

One day the Hebrew prophet Elijah met a poor widow gathering sticks at the town gate. This was during a severe drought. He asked her for a drink of water and a piece of bread.

"As surely as the Lord your God lives," she replied, "I don't have any bread—only a handful of flour in a jar and a little oil in a jug. I am gathering a few sticks to take home and make a meal for myself and my son, that we may eat it—and die." Elijah said to her, "Don't be afraid. Go home and do as you have said. But first make a small cake of bread for me from what you have and bring it to me, and then make something for yourself and your son. For this is what the Lord, the God of Israel says: 'The jar of flour will not be used up and the jug of oil will not run dry until the day the Lord gives rain on the land.'" She went away and did as Elijah had told her. So there was food every day for Elijah and for the woman and her family. For the jar of flour was not used up and the jug of

oil did not run dry, in keeping with the word of the Lord spoken by Elijah (1 Kings 17:12-16).

The truth of the widow's circumstances was that she and her son were about to starve. Elijah approaches and makes a bold, some might even say selfish, request: "I know you don't have much, but feed me first and then yourself and your son. Trust in the Lord; He will take care of you." This was not selfishness. Elijah was offering the woman a key. Once she took it, she had control. By faith and obedience she unlocked heaven's larder and brought down for herself and her family supernatural provision that sustained them until the drought ended. Her entire life and mind-set shifted from the circumstances of want and privation to a Kingdom perspective of unlimited abundance.

5.   **Keys represent authorization.** This is similar to number 1. Authorization means to be given the authority to act in the name or in the stead of whoever gave you the authority. "The boss authorized me to do this...." Possession of keys means that you are authorized to act in the name and authority of the one who owns the keys. By giving us the keys of the Kingdom of Heaven, Jesus gives us the authority to influence Heaven. He has authorized us to act in His name and on His authority to request whatever we wish that is in accordance with His will and purpose.

6.   **Keys represent power.** Whoever gives you keys gives you power at the same time. This is similar to control. You have control—power—over whatever you possess the keys for. If you know how to use the keys, whatever they unlock is at your disposal. The keys to your house give you the power to come and go and to allow or disallow others to enter. When Jesus gave us the keys to the kingdom, He gave us power in Heaven. Whatever we bind on earth affects Heaven; whatever we loose on earth affects Heaven; whatever we close on earth, Heaven closes.

Do we really have that much power as Kingdom citizens? Yes. The King does not want us to live as victims of the earth's system, so He has given us the ability to tap into a realm that is invisible but absolutely real and can literally affect the physical earth. This is why Christ was able to live an abundant life in times of crisis. He had power from Heaven. And He has given that power to us.

7. **Keys represent freedom.** When you have keys, you are free to go in and out. You are free to lock and unlock, to open and close. The keys of the Kingdom give us freedom from fear and all the other limiting emotions of an earthly system. I used to wonder why Jesus was so carefree, so calm, and so in control no matter what was happening around Him. It was because He had the key of freedom.

One day Jesus was asleep in the back of a boat while His cabinet (some of whom were fishermen) sailed it across the Sea of Galilee. As happens frequently on that body of water, a severe storm blew up suddenly. The storm was so fierce that even the experienced sailors aboard feared that the boat was going to sink. How could Jesus sleep through such a crisis? Their lives were in danger, and He was snoozing in the stern!

The disciples went and woke Him, saying, "Lord, save us! We're going to drown!" He replied, "You of little faith, why are you so afraid?" Then He got up and rebuked the winds and the waves, and it was completely calm. The men were amazed and asked, "What kind of man is this? Even the winds and the waves obey Him!" (Matthew 8:25-27).

Jesus said, "You of little faith, why are you so afraid?" In essence He was saying, "What's the matter? Where are your keys?" Then He took out a key, locked up the storm, and it stopped. In amazement, the disciples asked, "What kind of man is this?" Just a man with keys.

The keys of the Kingdom are the keys to ultimate truth, the knowledge of which brings true liberty. Jesus said:

If you hold to My teaching, you are really My disciples. Then you will know the truth, and the truth will set you free (John 8:31b-32).

By "teaching," Jesus is not referring so much to Scripture verses as much as the principles, laws, and precepts contained in those verses. Freedom comes in knowing the truth. Truth alone is not what sets you free. What sets you free is the truth *you* know. The keys of the Kingdom can bring you into the knowledge of the truth.

Seven Characteristics of Keys

1. **Keys are laws.** They are fixed, reliable standards that never change. When used correctly, they always work.

2. **Keys are principles.** When Jesus spoke of "the keys of the Kingdom," He wasn't talking about literal physical keys to open physical locks. The keys of the Kingdom are principles, systems that operate under fixed laws. When He gives us the keys, He gives us the principles by which the Kingdom of Heaven operates. We gain access to the systems that make the Kingdom of Heaven work. And once we learn the laws, the system, and the principles, all of heaven will be available to us.

3. **Keys are systems.** Every government runs on systems: the social system, the economic system, the political system, the educational system, the telecommunications system, etc. Knowledge of the systems and how they work is a key to power and influence. Control the systems and you control the government. Disrupt the systems and you disrupt the government. Destroy the systems and you destroy the nation. That's how powerful systems are. Even more, that's how powerful knowledge can be.

The systems of the Kingdom of Heaven are beyond the reach of those outside the kingdom and are in no danger of being disrupted or destroyed. Kingdom citizens, on the other hand, have access to those systems and can bring the influence of Kingdom systems to bear in earthly situations. That is why Kingdom citizens can rest confident in victory and success no matter what circumstances may suggest. So the most important thing any of us could do is to make sure that we are citizens of the Kingdom of Heaven.

4. **Keys activate function.** A car operates on gasoline. The "key" of gasoline activates the function of the car. Without gasoline, the car will not run no matter how many other keys you have. Likewise, a radio with no receiver cannot fulfill its function of converting radio waves into audible sound waves for you to hear. The "key" of a receiver is missing, and without it, the radio is only an empty, silent box. The box may be pretty, the glass clean and shiny, but it cannot fulfill its purpose because the key to activate its function is not there. To me, religion is like that attractive radio or that stylish but gas-less car that does not work. Like them, religion may look beautiful and impressive on the outside with all its regalia and traditions, but it has no keys and therefore lacks the ability and the power to activate Kingdom function.

The keys of the Kingdom activate Heaven so that we can fully enjoy our rights and privileges as Kingdom citizens. This is far more sure and secure than depending on the systems of the world for our enjoyment. On this point, Kingdom ambassador Paul counsels:

> *Command those who are rich in this present world not to be arrogant nor to put their hope in wealth, which is so uncertain, but to put their hope in God, who richly provides us with everything for our enjoyment* (1 Timothy 6:17).

The keys of the Kingdom allow us to enjoy all the rich and good things of God without measure.

5. **Keys initiate action.** Just as the key to a car initiates action by starting the engine, the keys of the Kingdom, when we know how to use them, initiate action in Heaven.

6. **Keys are the principles by which the Kingdom of God operates.** Not only are keys principles, but specifically, keys to the operation of the Kingdom. They give us access to the blueprints, the schematic, the flowcharts so that we can understand and appropriate the inner workings of the Kingdom of Heaven.

7. **Keys cannot be substituted by feelings, emotions, wishful thinking, or manipulation.** If you are locked out of your house without a key, no amount of begging or pleading or wishing will make that door open. If your car is out of gas, you can sit behind the wheel and dream and will all you want for it to move, but it will stay right where it is. Religion is built on feelings, emotions, wishful thinking, and manipulation. It is different with the Kingdom. The Kingdom of Heaven operates on keys. You can wish and feel and beg and plead all you want, but without the right keys, you will still be locked out of all the things God promised you because feelings don't open doors. Keys do.

In the world's system, you get ahead by killing, robbing, hurting, manipulating, climbing up on people, using people, stealing, gambling—any way you can. But in the Kingdom of Heaven, everything is reversed. To get ahead, you must do the opposite of what you do in the world. Instead of getting, you give; instead of hoarding, you release; instead of grabbing, you give up; instead of hating, you love; instead of every-man-for-himself, you show first regard to others. Yes, this is counterintuitive, but that is the way God's Kingdom works.

The Counterintuitive Nature of Keys

It is this very counterintuitive quality of the Kingdom of heaven that makes it so hard for the world to understand. The Kingdom of Heaven and the kingdoms of this world operate by completely opposite principles. People raised in the world's system cannot comprehend on their own the truly otherworldly nature of God's Kingdom. This is why Simon Peter could not recognize Jesus as the Messiah except by divine revelation.

This clash of systems is vividly illustrated by an encounter Jesus had one day with a rich young man who was interested in getting into the Kingdom.

> *As Jesus started on His way, a man ran up to Him and fell on his knees before Him. "Good teacher," he asked, "what must I do to inherit eternal life?" "Why do you call Me good?" Jesus answered. "No one is good—except God alone. You know the commandments: 'Do not murder, do not commit adultery, do not steal, do not give false testimony, do not defraud, honor your father and mother.'" "Teacher," he declared, "all these I have kept since I was a boy." Jesus looked at him and loved him. "One thing you lack," He said. "Go, sell everything you have and give to the poor, and you will have treasure in heaven. Then come, follow Me." At this the man's face fell. He went away sad, because he had great wealth. Jesus looked around and said to His disciples, "How hard it is for the rich to enter the kingdom of God!" (Mark 10:17-23).*

Once we get into the Kingdom and start functioning properly, we inevitably become prosperous. Prosperity is a natural product of Kingdom living. But we must live by the standards of the Kingdom in order to prosper in the Kingdom.

This rich young man had problems with Jesus' conditions because they ran counter to everything he had ever heard and believed about success and prosperity. He simply was not prepared for the counterintuitive command of Jesus to part with everything that he thought made him "somebody." This is why Jesus said that it is hard for a rich person to enter the Kingdom of God. The keys, the principles, the systems of the Kingdom are opposite to those of the world, from where they acquired their wealth.

In other words, *the opposite nature of Kingdom keys* makes it difficult for many people to understand the Kingdom. This young man had grown up in a world where you get by taking. He could not understand the principle of a Kingdom where you get by *giving*.

Additionally, it is *the power of ignorance of Kingdom keys* that can destroy us. Scripture says:

> *"My people are destroyed from lack of knowledge"* (Hosea 4:6a).

Because of ignorance of Kingdom keys, this rich young man did not know how to become richer, so he chose to hold onto wealth that literally was killing him rather than enter into wealth that could give him life. Coming into the Kingdom of God neither makes you poor nor requires you to become poor. But you have to know the keys.

This rich man thought he was rich, but was really poor because he did not understand the nature of true wealth. So he went away sad. A key principle of the Kingdom of Heaven, on the other hand, is this:

> *The blessing of the Lord brings wealth, and He adds no trouble to it* (Proverbs 10:22).

Once you get the keys of the Kingdom and learn how they work, the blessing of God will bring you wealth without sorrow. And He can do it in an instant if He is so inclined.

Another factor in the difficulty people have in understanding the Kingdom is *the danger of the fallen nature of human reasoning*. Man's rebellion against God resulted in a corrupted mind and conscience. The way most of us in this world pursue success and wealth and try to get ahead is completely contrary to the principles and laws that God designed into creation. But we are too blinded by our corrupt minds to see it. Like the rich young man, we assume that you must do certain things to succeed—climb the corporate ladder by walking on people's heads and stepping on their hands, hurt them, use them selfishly, scheme against them, betray them, lie, cheat, steal—whatever it takes to be a millionaire before the age of 40.

Then Jesus comes along and says, "If you want *real* wealth and *real* success, get rid of all of that. Give it back to the people you got it from and follow Me." The *attitude* of willingness to part with it all is as important, and perhaps more so, than the actual act. Remember, in the Kingdom of Heaven we are stewards, not owners.

Because of our fallen nature of human reasoning, the principles and keys of the Kingdom of God are completely foreign to the way we have been trained to think. That is why the first word Jesus said when He came to announce the Kingdom was, "Repent." Change the way you think.

Principles work but are not always understood. The rich young man simply could not see how following Jesus' instructions would get him what he wanted. He could not grasp the principle. The keys of the Kingdom work, but sometimes even after we learn how to use them, we don't understand how they work. They just do.

Principles are established by the manufacturer. Our Creator knows His creation. God knows what is best for us. But because of our fallen nature, we are dysfunctional creatures who believe either that there is nothing wrong with us or that whatever is wrong we can fix ourselves. Counterintuitive wisdom leads us to understand that the keys of the Kingdom, the principles under which the Kingdom operates, are also the keys to bringing the life, law, and culture of Heaven to earth, even when human logic or reasoning says otherwise.

Principles

1. Life in the Kingdom is really about returning to the governing authority of God in the earth and learning how to live and function in that authority.

2. The Kingdom of Heaven is not a secret society, but its keys have to be learned.

3. When you know the keys to the Kingdom secrets, you will never again say, "All I have is…."

4. Keys represent authority.

5. Keys represent access.

6. Keys represent ownership.

7. Keys represent control.

8. Keys represent authorization.

9. Keys represent power.

10. Keys represent freedom.

11. The keys of the Kingdom are the keys to ultimate truth, the knowledge of which brings true liberty.

CHAPTER TEN

Kingdom Concept #7
Understanding the
Kingdom Concept of Citizenship

The most awesome power and position of national privilege is citizenship. Citizenship is the most valuable asset of a nation and is not easily given because of its power and impact. All governments defend the right of citizenship with the same fervor because of its implications. Citizenship is not membership. Religions function on membership, while nations and kingdoms function on citizenship.

In recent months immigration has become a hot topic in some parts of the world. For example, there is rising concern among many Western Europeans that the continuing influx of Muslim immigrants from the Middle East will soon transform the entire religious, social, and cultural complexion of Europe. Recent sectarian riots in France over unemployment and in many other European countries over the publication of "blasphemous" cartoons of Muhammad have revealed that little cultural assimilation among those immigrants has occurred.

Of even greater concern, however, is the spectacle that has been going on in the United States over immigration. For months, debates have raged over the status of millions of illegal aliens, mostly from Mexico, who live and work in the U.S. Rallies in support of these illegals have drawn thousands out onto the streets. Some legislators have proposed granting all illegal aliens currently in the country immediate legal status and placing them on a short track to American citizenship. Others insist that the U.S. government detain and deport as many illegal immigrants as they can find and increase patrols at the U.S.-Mexican border to prevent further would-be immigrants from crossing over. There are even some who have seriously proposed building a fence along the entire 700-mile length of the border.

It seems that masses of people from south of the border are clamoring to get into the United States. Why? What draws them to risk life, capture, imprisonment, or deportation just to cross that border? It could be many things: better jobs, higher pay, better health care, greater opportunities, and an all-around better quality of life than they feel they can get in their home country. For many, it is the lure of even the *possibility* of citizenship in the most prosperous nation in the world.

I'm not trying to make a case either for or against the advantages or benefits of being an American citizen. My point here is that citizenship is a powerful draw. People are attracted to a nation that appears to promise a better life than the one they are living where they are. Some people even become desperate enough to do anything they have to do to become a part of that nation.

So the concept of citizenship is critical to understanding the nature of the Kingdom of heaven. As I've said before, all governments and kingdoms operate on governing laws and principles. Citizenship is necessary for the validity and legitimacy of any nation. Not only that, but *citizenship is the most sacred privilege of a nation.*

The Power and Privilege of Citizenship

Citizenship has great power as well as great privileges. That is why people are willing to risk their lives and cross borders even to the point of death to pursue the hope of citizenship. Citizenship is not only sacred, but sanctified—set apart. A citizen is part of an elite, privileged group. People who have lived as "subjects" of a foreign government rather than citizens understand this distinction much better than people who were born citizens. The same is true for people who have worked very hard to earn the privilege to become a naturalized citizen of their chosen country.

As a sacred privilege, citizenship is the most precious gift that any nation can give. That's why there are laws to protect people from it and protect it from people. Apart from native-born citizens, citizenship is neither awarded lightly nor obtained easily. And it shouldn't be. Citizenship is too precious a treasure to hand out indiscriminately like handbills.

When it comes to matters of citizenship, the Kingdom of God is no different from any other country. Remember, the Kingdom of God is not a religion. It is a government with a country. Heaven is that country, and Jesus Christ is its King. Referring to Christ, the ancient Hebrew prophet Isaiah wrote:

> *For to us a Child is born, to us a Son is given, and the **government** will be on His shoulders....Of the increase of His **government** and peace there will be no end. He will **reign** on David's throne and **over his kingdom**, establishing and upholding it with justice and righteousness from that time on and forever...* (Isaiah 9:6-7, emphasis added).

Like any other country, the Kingdom of God has the principle of citizenship. And, like the example of America above, once people know about the Kingdom, and once they understand what it is and what it has to offer, they *clamor* to get in. This is what Jesus was referring to when He said:

> *The Law and the Prophets were proclaimed until John. Since that time, the good news of the kingdom of God is being preached, and everyone is forcing his way into it* (Luke 16:16).

"Everyone is forcing his way into it." Once people learn about the Kingdom of God, they can't wait to get in! Picture in your mind all those would-be immigrants desperately clamoring to cross the border, and then you will see what Jesus meant.

Why then, someone might ask, do we not see people clamoring to get into the churches? Why does the church as a whole seem to have so little impact on our culture? The reason is simple—and sad. Most pastors don't understand the Kingdom, so they don't preach it or teach it. Consequently, most of the people in the churches don't understand the Kingdom either, so they don't model Kingdom living. My experience has been that once people know about the Kingdom and see it modeled, they *want* it!

Such is the *power* of the *lure of citizenship* in the Kingdom of Heaven.

Becoming a Kingdom Citizen

All nations, including kingdoms, have citizens. And all nations require immigration status. The Kingdom of God is no different. Every Kingdom citizen today is a naturalized citizen. We emigrated from a foreign country—a *"dominion of darkness"* (see Col. 1:13)—where we as a race had been "exiled" ever since Adam's rebellion in the garden of Eden. At that time, the human race lost citizenship in heaven. We lost our citizenship because we lost our Kingdom, and we lost our Kingdom because we lost our property—our territory. Don't forget that without territory, there is no kingdom; and without a kingdom, there can be no kingdom citizenship.

When Jesus Christ began His public ministry, He announced that the Kingdom of Heaven had arrived. That was the only message He preached. He brought back to earth the Kingdom we lost at Eden and gave us access to it again. We enter the Kingdom of heaven through the process that Jesus called being "born again" (see John 3:3)—changing our mind and turning from our rebellion against God, placing our trust in Jesus for the forgiveness of our rebellion, and acknowledging Him as Lord (Owner) of our lives. This "new birth" gets us into the Kingdom of Heaven.

Many believers call this "being saved," but I think it is more helpful here to think of the new birth as the "naturalization" process by which we become Kingdom citizens. The new birth makes us naturalized citizens of the Kingdom. It also "naturalizes" us in the sense that it returns us to our *original* "natural" state of authority and dominion over the earth as God intended from the start. When we become citizens of God's Kingdom, it means that we voluntarily align ourselves with a new government and a new country, embracing its language, its ideals, and its values.

The Kingdom constitution is explicit regarding our citizenship:

*Consequently, you are no longer foreigners and aliens, but **fellow citizens** with God's people and members of God's household* (Ephesians 2:19, emphasis added).

*But our **citizenship** is in heaven. And we eagerly await a Savior from there, the Lord Jesus Christ, who, by the power that enables Him to bring everything under His control, will transform our lowly bodies so that they will be like His glorious body* (Philippians 3:20, emphasis added).

*Giving thanks to the Father, who has qualified you to share in the inheritance of the saints in the kingdom of light. For He has rescued us from the dominion of darkness and **brought us into the kingdom of the Son** He loves* (Colossians 1:12-13, emphasis added).

Not only does the new birth make us citizens of Heaven, but our citizenship begins *immediately*. We are Kingdom citizens *right now*. Our citizenship is a *present reality*. We "*are*...fellow citizens with God's people." "Our citizenship is in Heaven." God "*has* brought us into the kingdom of the Son."

Why is this so important? Here's why: *Religion postpones citizenship to the future*. Religious leaders tell their people, "You *will* be a citizen... someday. You *will* be in the Kingdom...you *will* have joy later...you *will* be a full citizen. But not today. Not yet. The Kingdom has not yet come."

They are wrong. The Kingdom *has* come. Kingdom citizenship is never postponed. The Kingdom of God is present and functional on the earth *right now*. If you have been "born again," then you have been naturalized and are a Kingdom citizen *right now*. And that means that all the rights, benefits, and privileges of Kingdom citizenship are yours *right now*. You can enjoy your citizenship *right now*. You don't have to wait until some indefinite time in the future.

You can never appropriate what you postpone. That's what you call "locking up the Kingdom of God" to those who want to get in. It is for this reason that I am convinced that the greatest enemy of the Kingdom is religion. Religion keeps pushing the Kingdom away from people: "You can't get in now; you can't experience it now; you can't benefit from it now; wait until later." And so the people suffer. That is why so many religious people live defeated, destitute, and frustrated lives. They believe they have to wait for their "reward."

Dual Citizenship

Kingdom governments exercise jurisdiction over their citizens no matter where they are. One of the main purposes that nations maintain embassies in other countries is to provide assistance to their citizens who are living or traveling away from home. Once, in Africa, I had a problem and had to fly to London, England. The Bahamian embassy sent a chauffeured car to pick me up at the airport and put me up in a house.

A dear American friend of mine who was a missionary in Mozambique years ago spent the better part of a year in prison after the Communists took over the country. Upon his release, the American embassy paid for his plane ticket home, gave him $300 cash, and said, "Your wife will be waiting for you."

If you were to visit the Bahamas and happened to lose all your money or face some other crisis, all you would have to do is turn to your country's embassy and they would help you. That's what they are there for. One of the responsibilities of any government is to take care of its citizens, whether at home or abroad.

In a very real sense, that's what the church is (or what it is supposed to be): *an embassy*! The church is not a religious place. When Jesus established His *ecclesia*, He did not have a religious institution in mind. His purpose was to set up an embassy of His Kingdom—a place where Kingdom citizens (new and old) could receive aid, be trained in the ways, laws, language, and customs of the Kingdom, and be equipped with the Kingdom resources they need for effective life in the Kingdom colony on earth.

All Kingdom citizens carry dual citizenship. Most governments on earth allow dual citizenship, where citizens of one country may hold simultaneously legal citizenship in another. If you are an American or Canadian or German citizen, for example, you could become an official, legal citizen of the Bahamas without being required to give up your prior citizenship. Children born to citizens of one country who are living in another country generally become citizens of both countries.

It is no different with the Kingdom of Heaven. All Kingdom citizens are simultaneously citizens of the Kingdom of Heaven as well as citizens of the earthly nation of their birth or their naturalization. We don't give up our earthly citizenship when we become citizens of the Kingdom. And in the same way, we don't have to be in Heaven to benefit from heavenly jurisdiction. Our citizenship is constant, and the Kingdom government exercises jurisdiction over us wherever we are.

The Kingdom constitution says that we are *in* the world but not *of* the world. Even though we are in a foreign territory—actually, our government's colony—our registration is not here. When it says our citizenship is in Heaven, it means that our registration, our official documentation, is not on earth. When we are born again, our names are written in Heaven's "official registry" as valid confirmation that we are now citizens of Heaven, even though we still live in the colony. So even though we are physically away from the Kingdom "country," we are still citizens of the Kingdom.

When Jesus stood before Pilate, the Roman governor of Judea, Pilate asked Him, *"Are you the king of the Jews?"* (John 18:33b), to which Jesus answered:

> *My kingdom is not of this world. If it were, My servants would fight to prevent My arrest by the Jews. But now My kingdom is from another place* (John 18:36).

It is important to note here both what Jesus said as well as what He did not say. He said, *"My kingdom is not **of** this world"*; He did not say, "My kingdom is not *in* this world." He said, *"My kingdom is **from** another place"*; He did not say, "My kingdom is not *in this* place." As the official representative of the emperor, Pilate possessed kingly authority in Judea. Speaking as one king to another, Jesus acknowledged His kingship. In fact, He stated plainly to Pilate:

> *You are right in saying I am a king. In fact, for this reason I was born, and for this I came into the world, to testify to the truth"* (John 18:37b).

And what was that truth? The truth that the Kingdom of Heaven had arrived—the only message Jesus preached. So Christ's Kingdom was *in* the world but not *of* the world. It was *from* another place but also resident here on earth. It was here now, but it was not *from* here.

So all Kingdom citizens possess dual citizenship—in heaven and on earth. That status will continue until the day when the present heaven and earth pass away and the King re-creates them both. Then there will be no more separation because the time will have come when:

> *…the dwelling of God is with men, and He will live with them. They will be His people, and God himself will be with them and be their God* (Revelation 21:3).

On that day the government of heaven will exercise full dominion over the new earth under the co-regency of all kingdom citizens.

Invisible Citizenship

Someone may ask, "If the Kingdom of heaven is here now, why can't we see it? Why isn't there more evidence of it all around us?" The answer is very simple: We cannot see the Kingdom of Heaven because it is invisible. And so are its citizens. In fact, all colonial governments and citizens are invisible.

I grew up and have spent most of my life in the Bahamas. I am a Bahamian citizen who was born while the Bahamas was still part of the British Commonwealth. While I was growing up, I never visited England. I never visited Parliament or saw the queen. But like the rest of my countrymen, I knew they were there. After all, we sang their songs, wore their clothes, observed their laws, learned their history; but we never saw them. So the government was invisible...but it was real. Just look at us today: We speak English, we drive on the left side of the street, and carry on many customs and traditions that are the legacy of our years as part of the British Empire. In the Bahamas, the British government was invisible but also influential.

In the same way, the fact that the Kingdom of Heaven is invisible does not mean that it has no impact. Jesus taught this truth about the Kingdom more than once. On one occasion He illustrated it this way:

> *What shall I compare the kingdom of God to? It is like yeast that a woman took and mixed into a large amount of flour until it worked all through the dough* (Luke 13:20-21).

That's how yeast works—slowly but inexorably until all the dough feels its influence. Once mixed with the dough, the yeast is invisible, but if you think that means no impact, just try baking bread without it!

People have been debating the nature and timing of the coming of the Kingdom of heaven for centuries. It was no different in Jesus' day. One day He spoke of the invisibility of the Kingdom in response to a question from some of the religious leaders:

> *Once, having been asked by the Pharisees when the Kingdom of God would come, Jesus replied, "The kingdom of God does not*

come with your careful observation, nor will people say, 'Here it is,'
or 'There it is,' because the Kingdom of God is within you" (Luke
17:20-21).

The Kingdom of God is invisible. We cannot detect it simply by
observation. And if the Kingdom of God resides *within* its citizens, this
means that all Kingdom citizens are invisible also. We bear no physical
or outward signs that broadcast to the world, "I'm a Kingdom citizen!"
Our citizenship must become known in other ways.

One day in Ohio I shared an elevator with a lady who asked politely,
"How are you?"

"Fine," I replied, and we began to talk.

"Where are you from?" she asked.

"Why do you ask?" I answered.

"Because you have an accent."

She knew nothing about me until I *spoke.* There was no way for her
to tell just by looking at me that I was Bahamian. My citizenship was
invisible. It was my speech that clued her in to the fact that I was not
from her "neck of the woods." Citizenship is invisible. The only way you
can actually know someone is from a particular place is by listening to
them and observing their behavior over time.

The same is true with us as Kingdom citizens. There is no way for
people to tell by looking at us that we are citizens of the Kingdom. Our
language and our behavior should make that known to them. In other
words, they should recognize us by our *distinct culture.*

Culture is a product of the language, ideals, and values of a people or
a nation. Even though people cannot recognize us as Kingdom citizens
by our outward appearance, our distinctive language, ideals, and values
should give us away. Our culture should reflect and reveal our citizenship
as being *here* but not *from* here, as being *in* the world but not *of* the world.

Principles

1. Citizenship is the most sacred privilege of a nation.

2. Citizenship is the most precious gift that any nation can give.

3. Like any other country, the Kingdom of God has the principle of citizenship.

4. Every Kingdom citizen today is a naturalized citizen.

5. The new birth makes us naturalized citizens of the Kingdom.

6. Not only does the new birth make us citizens of heaven, but our citizenship begins immediately. We are Kingdom citizens right now. Our citizenship is a present reality.

7. Religion postpones citizenship to the future.

8. You can never appropriate what you postpone.

9. All Kingdom citizens carry dual citizenship.

10. All colonial governments and citizens are invisible.

11. The Kingdom of God is invisible.

12. All Kingdom citizens are invisible also.

13. Our culture should reflect and reveal our citizenship as being here but not from here, as being in the world but not of the world.

CHAPTER ELEVEN

Kingdom Concept #8
Understanding the
Kingdom Concept of Culture

Culture encompasses many things. Once you understand the culture of a people, you understand the people. Everything that makes a nation a nation and a people a people is wrapped up in their culture.

As we have already seen, for example, every country has *land*—territory. Without land there is no country. Historically, the land a people inhabits significantly influences the culture they develop. Desert dwellers, for instance, are unlikely to develop a maritime culture unless they live along the coast. Their culture will reflect the arid environment in which they live.

A second key component of every country is *language*. A country is not a country unless it has one major language. Many nations of the world have numerous sublanguages and dialects. But every nation always decides on one major language because language identifies you as a country. Language is the key to unity. It is also a key factor in a nation's culture.

Again, as we saw earlier, all countries have *laws*. Every nation draws up a body of laws that everyone must obey to ensure peace, order, and security for the citizens. Without law there is no country because the absence of law leads to chaos, and you can't run a country or maintain a stable government on chaos. The laws of a nation reflect the culture of that nation and vice versa. Culture and law each affect the other.

Every nation also utilizes specific and unique *symbols* to represent it and to help inspire unity, patriotism, loyalty, pride of nation, and a strong sense of national identity. The most familiar symbol of any nation is, of course, its flag. A nation's flag symbolizes its history, the sacrifices, suffering, and triumphs of its people, and what the people have constituted themselves to be. All of these things relate also to culture. Few national symbols are more powerful than the flag.

Another element that all nations share in common is a *constitution*. As we saw in Chapter Six, a constitution is a contract between the people and their government. In many ways a constitution is a cultural document because it contains in codified form the laws, ideals, and values of the people (or of the king, depending on who wrote it).

Furthermore, all nations have a *moral code*. A nation's moral code embodies the moral standards under which the people have agreed to live and by which they have chosen to govern themselves. In most cases, a moral code consists of both written and unwritten standards. The written standards are expressed through laws and statutes while the unwritten standards are transmitted primarily through traditions, customs, and culture. Respect other people's property; do not bear false witness in court; do not steal; do not murder; do not commit adultery—all of these are part of the moral code in virtually every nation and government on earth.

A seventh common characteristic of all countries is *shared values*. In order to have a country that runs effectively, the people must share the same values in common. The people as a whole must agree that they all value the same thing, such as life or peace or freedom.

Every nation also develops its own *customs*. Customs derive from a nation's shared values. A custom is a *customary* way of doing something, a behavioral pattern that is not only commonly accepted but also expected. Overall, customs generally are consistent throughout a nation, although there are many regional variations. Quite often a nation's customs are so distinctive that they become a point of identification for that nation, such as certain traditional manners of dress or kinds of foods.

Finally, there are *social norms*. These are similar to customs but have greater force and authority within society. Social norms are standards of speech, thought, and behavior that are accepted by the wide majority of the people as right and proper. Violate a custom and you may be thought eccentric; violate a social norm and you risk being ostracized.

All of these together—land, language, laws, symbols, constitution, moral code, shared values, customs, and social norms—comprise what we call *culture*.

What Is Culture?

So what is culture specifically? First of all, *culture is the act of developing the intellectual and moral faculties by education, expert care, and training*. In other words, culture is the developing of a people's intellectual capacities and moral awareness through a combination of formal instruction and informal modeling. Parents and society teach children the elements of the culture, and as the children learn and internalize those cultural elements, they begin to live them.

Secondly, *culture is the enlightenment and excellence of taste acquired by intellectual and aesthetic training*. Simply stated, we all come to think like the environment we grow up in. Our intellectual interaction with our environment literally produces a way of thinking in us that becomes our way of life, and so we become trained in our culture. None of us are born with a culture. We are born *into* a culture, but we are not born *with* a culture.

Culture may also be defined as the integrated pattern of human knowledge, belief, and behavior that depends upon man's capacity for learning and transmitting knowledge to succeeding generations. From a sociological perspective, culture is the customary beliefs, social forms, and material traits of a racial, religious, or social group. In the business world, culture defines the set of shared attitudes, values, goals, and practices that characterize a company or corporation.

As for a scientific definition, *culture means to grow in a prepared medium.* That's a powerful image. Each of us arrived on earth in a prepared medium—the country and culture of our birth. Immediately we began to grow in that medium, shaped and influenced by the customs, values, moral code, and social norms of our parents, community, and society. We learned the language and the laws. This growth medium is also where we learned our prejudices and our hatreds, our jealousy and our greed and our pride.

Then one day we discovered the Kingdom of Heaven. We were born again and became citizens of God's Kingdom. And that's where the challenge really began. After spending 20, 30 or 40 years in a certain medium that trained us to think a certain way, we suddenly find ourselves in a whole new culture—a new growth medium—with a whole lot of new things to learn and a whole lot of old things to unlearn. And therein lies the problem: How do we get rid of the old culture in our hearts and minds to live in the new one? That's the universal challenge for every dual citizenship believer.

For you see, culture is also what lies at the very center of the great cosmic conflict between the Kingdom of God and the kingdom of darkness. And earth is the battleground. The battle for earth is the battle for culture. And culture is the manifestation of the collective thinking of a people. In other words, whatever the people as a whole think collectively—their beliefs, values, ideals, etc.—becomes their culture. So whoever controls the minds of the people controls the culture. In fact, whoever controls the minds will create the culture.

The Bible says that as a man thinks in his heart, so is he (see Prov. 23:7 KJV). This means that the way we think determines who we become. In this context, the heart is the *mind*. And the Kingdom of God is a kingdom of the heart. Therefore, the King of Heaven is battling for the minds of the creatures He created in His own image.

Manifestations of Culture

Culture manifests itself in a number of ways.

1.   **Values.** Shared values are a defining characteristic of a culture and a nation. What we value reveals who we are. Our values reflect our character. Basically, *a value is a belief or conviction that is considered worthy in and of itself by a person or group.* It is a standard or ideal that regulates conduct or policy. Values also relate to one's personal philosophy. Our values define our attitudes, behavior, and view of the world. If we want to learn how to live in the culture of the Kingdom, we must learn the values of the Kingdom. Jesus the King articulated His value system at the very beginning of His public ministry:

Blessed are the poor in spirit, for theirs is the kingdom of heaven. Blessed are those who mourn, for they will be comforted. Blessed are the meek, for they will inherit the earth. Blessed are those who hunger and thirst for righteousness, for they will be filled. Blessed are the merciful, for they will be shown mercy. Blessed are the pure in heart, for they will see God. Blessed are the peacemakers, for they will be called sons of God. Blessed are those who are persecuted because of righteousness, for theirs is the kingdom of heaven (Matthew 5:3-10).

This particular portion of Jesus' teaching is commonly known as the "Beatitudes," or "blessed sayings," from the Latin word *beatus* (blessed). We could even call them the "Be-attitudes" because they describe the way Kingdom citizens should "be" in character, attitude, and behavior.

Values are extremely powerful and form the foundation for behavior. They guide the people of a nation in identifying what behavior is acceptable or unacceptable. Whether explicitly stated or unspoken yet recognized, values form the foundation of nations and profoundly shape the lives and daily experiences of their citizens. Society depends on certain values in order to function, such as cooperation and honesty. Businesses also depend for their function on such values as integrity, honor, fairness, and kindness.

2. **Priorities.** Culture manifests itself in the things we regard as most important. In other words, whatever we prioritize in life reveals our culture. If we prioritize the sanctity of marriage, our culture will reflect it with laws, customs, and social norms that strongly discourage and even penalize divorce, adultery, and other "marriage busters." Prioritizing the sanctity of human life will produce a culture that protects the elderly and the unborn and refuses to sanction the harvesting of human embryos for stem cell research.

Jesus got right to the heart of priorities when He said:

So do not worry, saying, "What shall we eat?" or "What shall we drink?" or "What shall we wear?" For the pagans run after all these things, and your heavenly Father knows that you need them. But seek first His kingdom and His righteousness, and all these things will be given to you as well (Matthew 6:31-33).

3. **Behaviors.** The way we behave reveals our culture; it's that simple.

4. **Standards.** The standards we apply in everyday life reveal whether we have a culture that indulges and

encourages mediocrity or a culture that inspires excellence. Do we take pride in the appearance of our houses and churches and businesses and cities and streets? Do we place a high premium on quality in all things? Or are we satisfied with just enough to get by? Either way, our standards reflect our culture. In fact, our culture will never rise higher than our standards.

5. **Celebration.** Our culture is revealed in the things we celebrate as well as in the manner that we celebrate. Are holidays and other celebrations opportunities for fun and laughter and togetherness as families, or excuses for drunkenness and other kinds of excess?

As Kingdom citizens, we need to take our cue from our King because His attitudes and responses reveal Heaven's culture. Whatever makes Jesus angry should make us angry and whatever makes Him happy should make us happy. Whatever fills Him with joy should make us joyful also and whatever brings Him sorrow should grieve our spirits as well.

6. **Morality.** The level of our moral conscience and consciousness reveals the level of our culture. Do we shrug our shoulders at adultery and other forms of infidelity? Do we turn a blind eye to pedophilia and other kinds of sexual abuse? Are we willing to "normalize" perversion in our society? Or are we committed to standing for, supporting, and promoting the highest standards of moral purity in every area?

7. **Relationships.** Who do we relate to? How do we relate to them? How do we treat people? How do we handle the destitute, those who are hurting, and those who are abused? What is our attitude toward the poor? There's a culture in Heaven that is revealed when poverty is around. When people are hungry, the culture of Heaven feeds them. When they are thirsty, the culture

of Heaven says, "I've got something for you to drink." Our culture is revealed in how well we take care of each other.

8. **Ethics.** Is honesty our best policy, or is honesty our *only* policy? If someone overpays us, do we keep the money or do we take it back? Kingdom ethics is always proactive. Jesus said, *"Do to others as you would have them do to you"* (Luke 6:31). This "rule" applies to every area of life.

Then Peter came to Jesus and asked, "Lord, how many times shall I forgive my brother when he sins against me? Up to seven times?" Jesus answered, "I tell you, not seven times, but seventy-seven times" (Matthew 18:21-22).

In response to Peter's question, Jesus pulled a number out of His hat to make His point. "Seventy-seven times" is not a literal figure; it is seven times extended indefinitely. In other words, in Kingdom culture, forgiveness is ongoing. We forgive as often as necessary, just as we would hope to be forgiven as often as necessary. Again, we take our cue from our King—as He has forgiven us, and keeps on forgiving us, so are we to do with others.

9. **Social norms.** Whatever is regarded as normal in our society reveals our culture. Is shacking up "normal"? Are out-of-wedlock pregnancies and births "normal"? Is cheating on taxes "normal"? Is corruption in government "normal"? Are honesty, integrity, and fidelity both at home and in the workplace "normal"? Is sexual purity "normal"?

What are the "norms" of the Kingdom of Heaven? Here are a few that Kingdom Ambassador Paul called "the fruit of the Spirit":

...love, joy, peace, patience, kindness, goodness, faithfulness, gentleness and self-control. Against such things there is no law (Galatians 5:22-23).

10. **Dress.** Culture also manifests itself in the way the people dress. How we dress speaks volumes about our values and ideals as well as how we feel about ourselves. All of these relate to culture.

Of course, since Kingdom citizenship and Kingdom citizens are invisible, there is no such thing as a Kingdom "uniform" or prescribed manner of dress. But there is such a thing as a certain demeanor that Kingdom citizens are to carry themselves with that identifies them as children of the King. Simon Peter's instructions to female citizens of the Kingdom applies equally in principle to every citizen:

> *Your beauty should not come from outward adornment, such as braided hair and the wearing of gold jewelry and fine clothes. Instead, it should be that of your inner self, the unfading beauty of a gentle and quiet spirit, which is of great worth in God's sight* (1 Peter 3:3-4).

11. **Foods.** Food has always been a cultural distinctive. Certain dishes, certain ingredients, and certain seasonings are associated with certain regions of the world or certain regions within nations. Curry is a distinctive of Indian cooking. Beans and rice are staples in Mexico. Hot dogs are undeniably American. In the Bahamas, it's peas and rice, conch chowder, and guava duff.

As Kingdom citizens on earth we need food to strengthen and nourish our bodies, but we also need heavenly food to nourish our spirits. Jesus said:

> *Man does not live on bread alone, but on every word that comes from the mouth of God* (Matthew 4:4b).

At another time, He told His inner circle of followers:

> *My food...is to do the will of Him who sent Me and to finish His work* (John 4:34).

12. **Permits.** We reveal our culture by what we permit. Remember, what we bind on earth is bound in heaven, and what we loose on earth is loosed in heaven. If we "loose" lewdness and immorality, those things will characterize our culture. If we "loose" corruption and dishonesty, we will have a corrupt and dishonest culture. On the other hand, if we "loose" love, joy, peace, patience, kindness, and the like, our culture will reflect these traits. As Kingdom citizens, we have the authority to bind and loose for the social, moral, and spiritual good of our fellowmen. This is why it is important for us to be involved in and to engage the popular culture and challenge it with the culture of Heaven.

13. **Acceptance.** Our culture is defined also by what we accept. More and more people who claim to be believers and even Kingdom citizens are buying into the popular culture to such a degree that by their language and lifestyle it is impossible to tell which Kingdom they belong to—the kingdom of the world or the Kingdom of heaven. The more often we hear about new cultural, social, or moral ideas, the more accepting we become until eventually it's not new to us anymore. We have accepted it, and now it has become a cultural norm. That's why we need to be always alert and ever careful to evaluate all the new ideas and philosophies that come down the line. Some of them may be fine. But many, perhaps most, will be contrary to the culture and values and ideals of the Kingdom of Heaven. When this is the case, as Kingdom citizens we have the duty and responsibility to refuse to accept them.

14. **Rejections.** On the other hand, our culture manifests also in what we reject. Modern popular culture has reached the point where it rejects almost nothing. An attitude of "anything goes" prevails in many circles. Political correctness rules the day with its calculated and deliberate determination to be nice to everybody, avoid hurting anyone's feelings, and refusing to

take a stand by judging anything as evil, immoral, or improper. Today's culture rejects the very idea of absolute standards; everything is relative. Kingdom culture, on the other hand, rejects relativism in favor of the absolute standard of the unchanging Word of God. If some things are right, then other things are wrong and must be rejected. Jesus said it this way:

He who is not with Me is against Me, and he who does not gather with Me scatters (Matthew 12:30).

We can't have it both ways. We can't play both ends against the middle. There is right and there is wrong, and Kingdom citizens must reject the wrong and embrace the right.

15. **Distinctions.** Culture manifests also in our distinctions. What distinguishes us from other cultures? What makes the Kingdom culture distinctive from the culture of the world? I'm not talking about outward things like clothing or hairstyle as much as inner qualities of character, values, and norms. Paul said:

For you were once darkness, but now you are light in the Lord. Live as children of light (Ephesians 5:8).

16. **Quality standards.** And finally, culture manifests in our standards of quality. God never does anything halfway, and neither should His children. In everything we do, Kingdom citizens should always be on the cutting edge of excellence, leading the way for everyone else rather than following in the world's wake. In Kingdom life we don't have to be perfect in what we do because we are imperfect people, but that is no excuse to accept shabby work, half-finished projects, or a just-enough-to-get-by attitude. Our King demands our best. And He deserves nothing less. For this very reason, it should be our joy to give our very best to the King...and to give it freely and willingly.

Principles

1. Once you understand the culture of a people, you understand the people.

2. Culture is the act of developing the intellectual and moral faculties by education, expert care, and training.

3. Culture is the enlightenment and excellence of taste acquired by intellectual and aesthetic training.

4. Culture is the integrated pattern of human knowledge, belief, and behavior that depends upon man's capacity for learning and transmitting knowledge to succeeding generations.

5. Culture is the customary beliefs, social forms, and material traits of a racial, religious, or social group.

6. Culture is the set of shared attitudes, values, goals, and practices that characterize a company or corporation.

7. Culture means to grow in a prepared medium.

8. The battle for earth is the battle for culture.

CHAPTER TWELVE

Kingdom Concept #9
Understanding the Kingdom
Concept of Giving to the King

The Bible is about a King, a Kingdom, and His kids.

As we have seen throughout this book, God is the King of a supernatural realm called Heaven that is invisible but very real. In fact, Heaven is more real than the natural realm in which we humans live, breathe, and have our being because it existed before the natural realm and is the source from which all nature originated.

God created the earth, bringing form out of formlessness and order out of chaos, not to leave it empty but for it to be inhabited (see Isa. 45:18). His original purpose and plan was to extend His heavenly Kingdom to the earth—to bring His invisible supernatural rule into the visible natural domain. It was for this reason that He created mankind—male and female—in His own image and clothed them in physical bodies of flesh and blood and bone made from the same stuff as the earth itself, that they might exercise dominion over the earth just as

197

He did in Heaven. They were to be His vice-regents, ruling in His name and under His authority.

King and kingdom are concepts that are of heavenly, not earthly origin. God chose these concepts to describe His plan and program for mankind and the earth. Thus, in order to understand God, we must understand the concept of kingship and kingdom. That has been the purpose and intent of this book.

Adam was created as king and ruler of the earth. This is only natural. God created man in His own image and likeness, and because God was a King, man was to be a king as well. As king of the earth, man possessed certain unique qualities and characteristics that set him apart as distinct from all other creatures on the earth. One of these qualities was self-determination. Man possessed the ability to reason—to frame his own thoughts and ideas and to make his own decisions. In this he was like his Creator. He was endowed also with the capacity for face-to-face, one-on-one intimate fellowship with God, a privilege that no other creature on earth enjoyed.

The Creator gave Adam the earth as his domain because a king is not a king unless he has territory over which to rule. Through inappropriate use of his power of self-determination, Adam rebelled against God and lost his earthly kingdom. Man's rule over the earth was usurped by an "unemployed cherub," a rebellious and fallen angel who had no right or authority to take it. Man became a slave in his own domain.

But the gifts and calling of God are irrevocable (see Rom. 11:29). God's original plan and purpose were still in place. Man's destiny was to rule the earth, so he had to get his Kingdom back. When the time was right in history, the King of Heaven sent His Son to earth to reestablish Heaven's rule here. He sent His Son to restore man to his earthly Kingdom. Jesus Christ entered the public eye proclaiming a simple but profound message: *"Repent, for the kingdom of heaven is near"* (Matt. 4:17b). As a human as well as the Son of God, Jesus had the authority both to restore the Kingdom and to rule it as King. Kingship was His birthright.

Kingship is always a matter of birthright or genealogy. You will remember that when Jesus stood before Pilate the morning He was crucified, and Pilate asked Him if He was the king of the Jews, Jesus answered, *"You are right in saying I am a king. In fact, for this reason I was born..."* (John 18:37b).

Jesus was not the only one to recognize His kingship. Even as early as His birth, there were those who knew who He was and why He had come:

> *After Jesus was born in Bethlehem in Judea, during the time of King Herod, Magi from the east came to Jerusalem and asked, "Where is the one who has been born king of the Jews? We saw His star in the east and have come to worship Him"* (Matthew 2:1-2).

The coming of Jesus Christ as King demonstrates another important characteristic of God: He is a *giver*. First, He gave man the earth to rule. Then, after man lost his Kingdom, God gave His Son so that He could get man's Kingdom back. Jesus gave Himself, even to the point of death, to salvage man from the effects and consequences of his rebellion against God. In the coming of Jesus, and throughout the Bible we see over and over that giving is a fundamental principle of the Kingdom of Heaven.

God is a *giver*. In fact, His honor as King of Heaven demands a gift. As God, He gives because it is His nature. As Kingdom citizens, we give because we are like Him, created in His image and likeness, and because giving is a proper way to honor a king.

The Six Royal Kingdom Principles of Giving

1. **The power of kings is displayed in their wealth.** The wealthier the king, the greater his power (or at least the perception of his power in the eyes of others). This is why kings are always seeking to increase their wealth and expand their territory. The most obvious way that wealth displays a king's power is in his ability to give

generously, lavishly, and even recklessly of his wealth to his citizens as well as to outsiders who visit his kingdom.

Kings who rule over lands that are sparse in resources and whose citizens are poor are judged to be poor kings, lacking in power and influence and therefore dismissed as unimportant. They may even be perceived as unable or unwilling to take proper care of their citizens and subjects. Poor kings, therefore, develop a poor reputation, which brings us to the second principle.

2.   **The purpose for a king's wealth is to secure his reputation—his glory.** Every conscientious king wants to be known as good, benevolent, magnanimous, and just. He is constantly concerned for the complete welfare of his people. He wants to be able to show the world that he can provide his citizens with anything and everything they need. Want in a kingdom is a shame to the king.

So a king's reputation is tied to his ability to take care of his citizens, and that ability is directly related to his wealth. A king whose people are secure in his benevolent provision will be loved by his people, respected by other kings and rulers, and will enjoy a stable and secure reign. His reputation is firmly established, and his glory shines to all around.

3.   **The glory of a king is his power to out-give another king.** This is another reason why wealth is important to a king. Kings are deeply and continually concerned with their reputations, and no king likes the thought that another king might be richer, more benevolent, or more giving than he. Consequently, kings will give freely in response to a gift given to them, or from pure beneficence, often wildly out of proportion to the value of the gift received or the merit of the recipient.

This is definitely a characteristic of the King of Heaven. As owner of literally everything, God is the richest King that was, is, or ever will be.

No one can out-give God. And He gives lavishly without regard to our merit or our ability to repay. Don't forget that Jesus assured us that it was His Father's pleasure to give us the Kingdom. And He did not demand that we make ourselves "worthy" first.

4. **Giving places a demand on the king's wealth.** Wealth that is not used for anything serves no purpose. Righteous and benevolent kings do not seek riches simply for their own enrichment and pleasure. They don't acquire wealth just so they can sit atop the pile and say, "Look at me! See how rich I am!" Good kings use their wealth to bring prosperity to their people and improve the quality of their lives. This way the king's riches do not stagnate or rot away. In keeping with a fundamental principle of wealth-building, good kings know how to make their wealth work for them—they give it away in order to receive more. It is a principle of reciprocity—giving begets giving.

The principle of reciprocity works both ways. Giving to a king places a demand on his wealth because a king cannot allow himself to be out-given. Whatever he receives as a gift he must return in multiplied form. This brings us to the fifth principle of giving.

5. **Giving requires a response from the king.** When you give to a king, he is obligated not only to respond to your gift but also to exceed it. When the queen of Sheba visited King Solomon of Israel, her gifts to him of spices, large quantities of gold and precious stones, was fitting protocol. However, she was not prepared for the magnitude of wealth she found in Solomon's court:

When the queen of Sheba saw all the wisdom of Solomon and the palace he had built, the food on his table, the seating of his officials, the attending servants in their robes, his cupbearers, and the burnt offerings he made at the temple of the Lord, she was overwhelmed. She said to the king, "The report I heard in my own country about your achievements and your wisdom is true. But I did not believe these things until I came and saw with my own eyes. Indeed, not even half was told me; in wisdom and wealth you have far exceeded the report I heard....And she gave the king 120 talents of gold, large quantities of spices, and precious stones. Never again were so many spices brought in as those the queen of Sheba gave to King Solomon....King Solomon gave the queen of Sheba all she desired and asked for, **besides what he had given her out of his royal bounty** (1 Kings 10:4-7,10,13a, emphasis added).

As lavish as the queen's gifts to Solomon were, his gifts to her in return far exceeded hers to him.

The King of Heaven is the same way. When we give to Him, He responds in kind but in much greater measure. Jesus said:

Give, and it will be given to you. A good measure, pressed down, shaken together and running over, will be poured into your lap. For with the measure you use, it will be measured to you (Luke 6:38).

We can never out-give God. Give, and He will give abundantly and overflowing in return. It's a principle of His Kingdom. Besides, His reputation and glory are at stake.

6.   **Giving to a king attracts His wealth to the giver.** Giving begets giving. This principle works both ways. Kings give away wealth in order to gain more wealth. But when we give to the King, it begets giving back to us because our generosity attracts the King's wealth to us.

This is directly related to the concept of stewardship versus ownership. As long as we feel we own what we have, we tend to cling to it and hold it close to our chest. In that posture, it is impossible to receive more. We can't receive anything with closed fists and clenched fingers. On the other hand, when we approach the King open-handed with our things, not only can we lay them at His feet as a gift, but we are also in a posture to receive. Giving to the King attracts His wealth because He is a giver and is attracted to those who share a like spirit.

Seven Reasons to Give to a King

1. **Royal protocol requires that a gift must be presented when visiting a king.** This is why the queen of Sheba brought such lavish gifts to King Solomon even though he was richer than she was. It was royal protocol. He would have done the same had he visited her.

This protocol of presenting a gift to the king reflects a principle of heaven. When God gave Moses the Law for the nation of Israel, He made it clear that whenever the people came before the Lord, they were to bring an offering or a sacrifice of some kind, depending on the occasion. They were never to approach Him with nothing. God commanded Moses:

And none shall appear before Me empty-handed (Exodus 34:21b NKJV).

The principle still applies. We should always approach the King with a gift of some kind to offer: a tithe or 10 percent of our income, praise, thanksgiving, worship; just not empty-handed. The best gift we can give Him is our heart and life, freely and completely.

2. **The gift must be fitting for the king.** Worse than approaching a king with no gift is to bring a gift unworthy of him. An inappropriate or inadequate gift amounts to an insult to the king. It shows that the giver does not properly respect the king or his authority. This is why the sacrificial laws of the Jews (which prefigure the sacrifice of Christ, the perfect Lamb of God who took away the sin of the world [see John 1:29]). stipulated that only spotless, unblemished, unflawed animals could be offered in sacrifice. The people were giving a gift to the King, and their gift had to be worthy of Him.

When King David of Israel set out to build an altar to the Lord, he sought to buy a threshing floor owned by a man named Araunah as the site. Araunah graciously offered to give the threshing floor to David for his purposes:

> *But the king replied to Araunah, "No, I insist on paying you for it. I will not sacrifice to the Lord my God burnt offerings that cost me nothing." So David bought the threshing floor and the oxen and paid fifty shekels of silver for them"* (2 Samuel 24:24).

David was trying to stop a plague in the land caused by his own disobedience to God. After he built the altar and made sacrifices, God responded to his prayers and stopped the plague.

Give a gift to the King that is worthy of Him. Don't offer something that costs you nothing.

3. **The gift reveals our value or "worth-ship" of the king.** The quality of what we offer the King and the attitude with which we offer it reveal much more than our words do of the value or worthiness we attach to Him. Quality doesn't mean expensive or fancy necessarily, but it does mean offering our very best. And our gift does not necessarily have to be of monetary value. Of much greater value to the King is the gift of a heart that seeks first His Kingdom and His righteousness. The Hebrew prophet Isaiah records the Lord's complaint against His people who devalue His "worth-ship":

> *The Lord says: "These people come near to Me with their mouth and honor Me with their lips, but their hearts are far from Me. Their worship of Me is made up only of rules taught by men* (Isaiah 29:13).

Our gifts to the King should always be offered from a sincere heart and a humble recognition of His greatness and awesome majesty.

4. **Worship demands a gift and giving is worship.**
   "Worth-ship" is where we get "worship." To worship
   the King means to ascribe worth or worthiness to Him.
   And, as we have already seen, that always involves
   bringing Him a gift. There is no genuine worship without gift-giving. But giving is itself an act of worship,
   and worship is always fitting for the King. The Magi
   who saw His star in the east understood this, which is
   why they brought gifts when they came to find Him:

On coming to the house, they saw the child with His mother Mary, and they bowed down and worshiped Him. Then they opened their treasures and presented Him with gifts of gold and of incense and of myrhh (Matthew 2:11).

Worship demands a gift, but it may be a gift of praise, a gift of thanksgiving, a gift of confession, a gift of surrender, a gift of forgiveness, or a gift of a tender and obedient heart as well as a monetary gift.

5. **Giving to a king attracts his favor.** Kings are attracted
   to people who give with a willing and grateful spirit.
   Like anyone else, a king likes to know he is loved and
   appreciated. The King of Heaven is the same way. The
   Giver is attracted to the giver and extends His favor.
   Gifts open doors to blessings, opportunities, and
   prosperity:

A gift opens the way for the giver and ushers him into the presence of the great (Proverbs 18:16).

Those who know the protocol of giving gain access to the throne room, while those who do not, remain standing outside the gate.

Giving from a generous heart with no thought or expectation of return particularly attracts the King's favor because that is the attitude closest to His own. And He rewards that kind of spirit:

Anyone who receives a prophet because he is a prophet will receive a prophet's reward, and anyone who receives a righteous man because he is a righteous man will receive a righteous man's reward. And if anyone gives even a cup of cold water to one of these little ones because he is My disciple, I tell you the truth, he will certainly not lose his reward (Matthew 10:41-42).

To "receive" a prophet or a righteous man means to care for and supply that person with no expectation of repayment. Giving with no ulterior motive and with no strings attached—that is the kind of giving that attracts the favor of the King.

6. **Giving to a king acknowledges his ownership of everything.** Remember, kings are also lords; they own everything in their domain. So giving to a king is simply returning to him what is already his. That's why in the Kingdom of Heaven we are always stewards and never owners.

This truth is embodied in the Bible in the principles of the first-fruits and the tithe. Every harvest the Jews were required to bring the "firstfruits" of the harvest and offer them to the Lord. The same was to be done with all the firstborn of the animals: sheep, goats, cattle. In addition, a tithe—10 percent—of one's increase, one's income and produce, was to be given to the Lord. All of this was for the purpose of recognizing God's ownership—His Lordship—of everything and His benevolence and love in allowing them to use and prosper from His resources.

These same principles apply today, at least in the spirit of acknowledging God's ownership. Kingdom citizens should still give the tithe regularly as an act of faith and of worship in recognizing not only God's ownership but also His daily provision of our needs as well as abundant blessings.

7. **Giving to a king is thanksgiving.** One of the best ways to express gratitude is with a gift. Gratitude expressed is in itself a gift. Look at the word "thanksgiving." Turn it

around and you have, "giving thanks" or "giving gratitude." Everyone likes to know they are appreciated. Sometimes the best gift we can give a person is simply to express heartfelt thanks for a gift given or a kindness received. God is the same way. Expressing our thanks to God from a sincere heart for His blessings, kindness, and favor toward us is to offer Him a gift that He receives with delight.

Five Reasons to Give

Giving is natural for kings. As Kingdom citizens and children of the King, we too are kings. That being the case, several principles follow:

1. If we all are kings, then we should give to each other. Remember, you never approach a king without a gift.

2. When we give to the Body, we give to Christ the King. Because Christ lives in us through the Holy Spirit, every time we give to each other, we are giving to Him.

3. Every time we meet one another, giving should be automatic. If we are to be like our King, who created us in His image and likeness, a giving spirit should be second nature for us.

4. The wise men knew there was a greater King on earth. That is why they brought Him gifts and worshiped Him. He is still on earth—in the hearts and lives of His citizens. So whenever we give, we do so as if giving to Him.

5. When you give to a king, you make a demand on what he possesses. Giving begets giving. When we give to the King of Heaven, we obligate Him to give in return. This is not a presumptuous statement but the expression of a principle He established. When we give, He gives; when we withhold, He withholds.

The Ultimate Gift

The ultimate and greatest gift the King wants from us is summed up in these words:

Love the Lord your God with all your heart and with all your soul and with all your strength (Deuteronomy 6:5).

Giving activates royal obligation.

Give Him *your* life and receive *His* life.

...remembering the words the Lord Jesus Himself said: *"It is more blessed to give than to receive"* (Acts 20:35).

Principles

1. Giving is a fundamental principle of the Kingdom of Heaven.

2. God is a giver.

3. The power of kings is displayed in their wealth.

4. The purpose for a king's wealth is to secure his reputation—his glory.

5. The glory of a king is his power to out-give another king.

6. Giving places a demand on the king's wealth.

7. Giving requires a response from the king.

8. Giving to a king attracts his wealth to the giver.

9. Royal protocol requires that a gift must be presented when visiting a king.

10. The gift must be fitting for the king.

11. The gift reveals our value or "worth-ship" of the king.

12. Worship demands a gift and giving is worship.

13. Giving to a king attracts his favor.

14. Giving to a king acknowledges his ownership of everything.

15. Giving to a king is thanksgiving.

16. Giving begets giving.

17. Giving activates royal obligation.

18. Give Him your life and receive His life.

Devotional Journal

The Priority of the Kingdom

Look at the birds of the air; they do not sow or reap or store away in barns, and yet your heavenly Father feeds them. Are you not much more valuable than they? Who of you by worrying can add a single hour to his life? (Matthew 6:26-27)

TODAY'S DEVOTION

The greatest secret to living effectively on earth is understanding the principle and power of priorities. Life was designed to be simple, not complicated, and the key to simplifying life is prioritization.

Priority is defined as:

- The principal thing.
- Putting first things first.
- Establishing the most important thing.
- Primary focus.
- Placing in order of importance.
- Placing highest value and worth upon.
- First among all others.

When your priorities are correct, you preserve and protect your life. Failure to establish correct priority causes you to waste your two most important commodities: your time and your energy. We should want to know what our priority in life should be so that we can live effectively. Most of the people in the world are driven by incorrect priorities that occupy and control their entire lives. These are:

1. Water.
2. Food.
3. Clothes.
4. Housing.
5. Protection.
6. Security.
7. Preservation.
8. Self-actualization.
9. Significance.

Meeting human needs is the premise of all religions. Priority in religious prayers and petitions is for personal needs. Human needs drive religion. Much of what we call "faith" is nothing more than striving for these things.

(Excerpt: *Kingdom Principles*, Chapter 1)

QUESTIONS

1. If "the greatest secret to living effectively on earth" is understanding the principle and the power of priorities," how effective is your life? Do you tend to live by prioritization or do you live by circumstances?

2. How do you determine your daily choices for the competing alternatives to your limited time? Are you someone who does not plan much, or do you plan and find yourself unable to proceed with the plan, or are you someone who plans and executes well? How do your daily choices affect your life currently?

3. Look over the definitions ascribed to the word priority above. How do these definitions help speak to your own life choices? How do they bring quality or the lack of quality to your daily life?

4. If "the greatest tragedy in life is not death but life without purpose—life with the wrong priorities," how tragic has your life been thus far? Do you sense your purpose in life in most everything you do? Why or why not?

5. Look at the list of needs outlined above. Rank these in order of how they press within your world. How much do you dwell on the top two or three needs? How much of your prayer life is affected by these needs?

MEDITATION

"If our priorities determine the quality of life and dictate all of our actions and behavior, then it is essential that we understand and identify our priorities. The greatest tragedy in life is not death but life without a purpose—life with the wrong priorities. Life's greatest challenge is in knowing what to do. The greatest mistake in life is to be busy but not effective—to be successful in the wrong assignment."

Take time before the Lord to ask forgiveness in any area He reveals where you have been led by circumstances more than by priorities. Ask Him to identify wrong priorities and bring to light those that He desires you to have.

DAY 2

The Priority of God

Seek first the kingdom of God and His righteousness, and everything you need for life will be added to you (Matthew 6:33).

TODAY'S DEVOTION

G
od established His priority at the beginning of creation and made it clear by His own declaration to mankind:

Therefore I tell you, do not worry about your life, what you will eat or drink; or about your body, what you will wear. Is not life more important than food, and the body more important than clothes? (Matthew 6:25)

The word *worry* means to consume in thought, to establish as our first interest, mental preoccupation, priority concern, fretting, fear of the unknown, and to rehearse the future over which we have no control.

Our self-worth is more important than our basic needs and should never be sacrificed for the sake of those needs.

So do not worry, saying, "What shall we eat?" or "What shall we drink?" or "What shall we wear?" For the pagans run after all these things, and your heavenly Father knows that you need them (Matthew 6:31-32).

The word *pagans* here implies that religion should not be motivated by the base drives of human needs for food, water, clothing, shelter, and the like.

God's number-one priority for mankind is that we discover, understand, and enter the Kingdom of Heaven.

(Excerpt: *Kingdom Principles*, Chapter 1)

QUESTIONS

1. How much do you worry about your basic life issues? To check this, look at any area where someone else would consider your actions more extreme than the average person's. How can you submit your areas of worry to the Lord?

2. How does worry establish itself in your life? Does it come suddenly or grow step by step? What can you do to prevent worry from coming into your mind and heart?

3. Describe your self-worth. Have you ever sacrificed your self-worth for your basic needs? Why should this never happen?

4. Why are pagans associated with the worry over basic needs? What statement do we make as Christians when we worry the same as the pagans? How should Christians differ from pagans in this as a testimony to the Kingdom of God?

5. Describe the process of discovery, understanding, and entering the Kingdom of Heaven through your own experience. How do we continue this experience forward in our lives?

MEDITATION

"Jesus suggests that there must be something about the Kingdom that all of mankind has missed and misunderstood. If everything we pursue and strive for to live and survive are found in the Kingdom, then we have been misguided and perhaps have imposed on ourselves unnecessary hardship, stress, and frustration."

Therefore do not worry about tomorrow, for tomorrow will worry about itself. Each day has enough trouble of its own (Matthew 6:34).

Take time to consider what you have missed or misunderstood about the Kingdom. Ask the Lord to reveal to you anything that He needs you to see to understand how His Kingdom works. Ask Him to give you the eyes to see that His Kingdom can provide what you need.

God's Priority Assignment for Humankind

Blessed are those who hunger and thirst for righteousness, for they will be filled (Matthew 5:6).

TODAY'S DEVOTION

Jesus instructs us to seek first the Kingdom. Jesus tells us to also seek the righteousness of the Kingdom. In essence, righteousness describes the maintenance of the rightly aligned relationship with a governing authority so as to qualify for the right to receive governmental privileges. Jesus emphasizes the Kingdom and the need to be righteous so that you can receive "all things added unto you." This promise includes all your physical, social needs, emotional, psychological, financial, security needs, and a sense of self-worth and purpose.

Therefore, God established only two priorities for mankind: *the Kingdom of God and the righteousness of God.*

All of us are seeking the Kingdom even if we all don't realize it. Ignorance of the Kingdom concept makes it difficult to understand fully the message of the Bible.

The secret to a full and fulfilled life is discovery, understanding, and application of the Kingdom of Heaven on earth. Religion postpones the Kingdom to a future experience. God's desire for you is that you enter the Kingdom life *now* and experience, explore, apply, practice, and enjoy living with the benefits, promises, and privileges of Heaven on earth.

(Excerpt: *Kingdom Principles*, Chapter 1)

QUESTIONS

1. What does seeking the Kingdom first mean to you? What do you think it means to seek the righteousness of the Kingdom? How do you do this in a practical way?

2. In your opinion, what does the righteousness of the Kingdom include? What aspects of righteousness do you see in the Church today? What aspects are needed?

3. When Jesus tells us that all things will be added to us if we seek His Kingdom and righteousness first, do you think most Christians truly believe this? Why or why not? Do you struggle finding the faith to believe this to be true? Why or why not?

4. Why is it true that "all of us are seeking the Kingdom even if we all don't realize it"? Does this mean that non-Christians are seeking the Kingdom? What shows us that they are doing so? How can the knowledge of this fact help us to be ready to share with non-believers?

5. How would you explain the difference between the way religion deals with the Kingdom and the way a relationship with Christ explains the Kingdom? How does your life in the Kingdom bring you fulfillment?

MEDITATION

*"The concept of 'kingdom' was not invented by
mankind but was the first form of government
introduced by the Creator. Man's original assignment
from God was a Kingdom assignment: 'Let them
have dominion over...the earth.' Yahweh, the King,
extended His heavenly Kingdom to earth through
His offspring, man. This is the wonderful story and
message of the Bible—not a religion, but a
royal family."*

How do you feel being part of a royal family? Take time to
understand what this means from God's perspective.

The Kingdom of God Versus
the Governments of Man

The creation waits in eager expectation for the sons of God to be revealed. For the creation was subjected to frustration, not by its own choice, but by the will of the one who subjected it, in hope that the creation itself will be liberated from its bondage to decay and brought into the glorious freedom of the children of God (Romans 8:19-21).

TODAY'S DEVOTION

Ninety percent of all the national and international problems facing our world today are the result either of government or religion. This includes global hunger, health epidemics, wars, terrorism, racial and ethnic conflicts, segregation, nuclear tension, and economic uncertainty.

The need for government and order is inherent in the human spirit and is a manifestation of a divine mandate given to mankind by the Creator. Man was created to be a governor and ruler, and therefore, it is his nature to seek some authority mechanism that would bring order to his private and social world.

Man's need for some formal government structure is an outgrowth of his need for social order and relationship management. This need begins in the smallest prototype of society, the family, and extends all the way to the manifestation of national expressions of constitutional order.

The mandate of the Creator for mankind was rulership and dominion. Therefore, the first command given to man by his Creator was to establish a "government" on the earth to destroy chaos and to maintain order. Government is God's solution to disorder.

Some governments are better than others, but *all* are inferior to God's government—the Kingdom of Heaven.

(Excerpt: *Kingdom Principles*, Chapter 2)

QUESTIONS

1. "Ninety percent of all the national and international problems facing our world today are the result either of government or religion." Have you seen this to be true in the world you observe? Think through current events and see if 90 percent are attributable to government or religion.

2. Have you ever met anyone who did not respond to order and government at all? Do you believe that "government and order is inherent in the human spirit"? If this is true, why do you think we sometimes rebel against it?

3. How does the need for social order manifest itself in your life? Do you find your relationships are comfortably managed for the most part or do you see them as being more chaotic and unpredictable?

4. Where do you think national pride or patriotism comes from in terms of man's need for government and social order? Does this explain why we can have patriotism despite the failings of our government? Why or why not?

5. Do you think your dominion or rulership is an option? How does your answer speak to those who say some are followers and some are leaders?

MEDITATION

"Governing is serious business. When man rejected Heaven's government, he became the source of his own governing program. The results ever since have proven that we need help. The Creator's intent was to administrate earth government from Heaven through His image (nature) in man and thus manifest His nature and character on earth. God's government is government by corporate leadership. [It is] the theocratic order of a King over kings as partners in governing!"

Over what has God given you to govern? Do you tend to govern according to your own governing program or as a corporate leadership with God? Take time to contemplate where you lack God's leadership in the areas of your own rulership.

DAY 5

The Government of Man Versus the Government of God

Then God said, "Let Us make man in Our image, in Our likeness, and let them rule [or have dominion] over the fish of the sea and the birds of the air, over the livestock, over all the earth, and over all the creatures that move along the ground" (Genesis 1:26).

TODAY'S DEVOTION

L et us look at some of man's attempts at government.

Feudalism

Feudalism describes a governing or ruling system that was established by virtue of the power of ownership. Feudalism was a derivative of the original government established under Adam, who was made the landlord of the earth. Feudalism puts the authority that belongs to the King of Heaven into the hands of unrighteous humans.

Dictatorship

Dictatorship is the form of government derived from the concept of "divine authority." A dictatorship is government that concentrates its power and authority in the hands of one individual who wields absolute authority unrestricted by laws, constitution, or any other social/political factor.

Communism

Communism is man's attempt to control land and people by the exercise of dictatorship. Communism attempts to reestablish the Kingdom of Heaven on earth as given to Adam, but without the involvement of the source of creation Himself. In essence, communism is an attempt to establish a kingdom without righteousness.

Socialism

Socialism substitutes the state for the king and attempts to control society for the benefit of society. Absolute power corrupts absolutely, and the state loses its concern for the individual as it becomes more obsessed with its own power.

(Excerpt: *Kingdom Principles*, Chapter 2)

QUESTIONS

Give the pros and cons to the concepts of the governmental systems and your take on why they fail.

System	Pros	Cons	Why They Fail
Feudalism			
Dictatorship			
Communism			
Socialism			

Looking at your answers within the chart above, can you make any conclusions about how people need to look at the type of governments they erect?

MEDITATION

"Government is about order, influence,
administration, distribution, protection, maintenance,
accountability, responsibility, and productivity.
Governing incorporates the concepts of both power
and authority. Both authority and power must be in
balance for government to be successful. Authority
has to do with responsibility while power has to do
with ability. Authority has to do with empowerment;
power focuses on exercising authority. Authority gives
power its legality."

Think about those over whom you govern, whether in your job, family, ministry, or other social activity. Rate yourself in the areas mentioned above: order, influence, administration, distribution, protection, maintenance, accountability, responsibility, and productivity. Where do you need to improve?

Government and God: Democracy

"Now if you obey Me fully and keep My covenant, then out of all nations you will be My treasured possession. Although the whole earth is Mine, you will be for Me a kingdom of priests and a holy nation." These are the words you are to speak to the Israelites (Exodus 19:5-6).

TODAY'S DEVOTION

Democracy is the best form of civil government as we know it because of its basic tenets and because of the checks and balances of the system. It is built on the premise and principle of the "majority rule" and the protection of individual rights. Despite its advantages and benefits, however, democracy does come with a few crucial defects. One such defect is its fundamental and major principle of "majority rule." This defect is critical because even though it gives power to the majority of the people, at the same time it places morality, values, and the standards for law at the mercy of the majority vote, thus legitimizing the majority's values, desires, beliefs, aspirations, and preferences.

If the power of democracy is in the people, then "we the people" become the sovereign of our lives and corporate destiny, and become our own providential ruler and god. This is the reemergence and manifestation of the age-old philosophy of humanism.

In essence, the problem with democracy—rule of the people— is that the vote of many can be the wrong vote. Another weakness of democracy is that it is not absolute. It can be easily influenced by the changing culture.

(Excerpt: *Kingdom Principles*, Chapter 2)

QUESTIONS

1. What are the benefits of democracy that you particularly enjoy? What are some benefits that are not so easily seen but nevertheless enjoyed?

2. What are the problems with democracy that you find particularly disturbing? What are some of the hidden problems that many people do not understand?

3. In a democracy, what do you think God's requirement is to participate within the governing structure and its authority? What limits do we have?

4. How well do you participate within the structure of government over you? Are you active or inactive? Are you informed or unknowledgeable? What do you think God's desires are in terms of your involvement?

5. Have you helped to fight against the problems that exist within a democratic government? Have you fought against humanism in any way? Have you worked to keep a moral basis for our government?

MEDITATION

"Democracy cannot succeed without God any more than communism can succeed without God. God is not subject to our politics, nor can He be, but He has created His own political system and governmental structure which is far superior to all forms of earthly government. From the Creator's perspective, life is politics, and He is the essence of life."

If, from God's perspective, life is politics, then how involved should we be in earthly politics? What is God asking you to do to be part of His Kingdom's political system?

DAY 7

The Return of the King and His Kingdom

From that time on Jesus began to preach, "Repent, for the kingdom of heaven is near" (Matthew 4:17).

TODAY'S DEVOTION

We need to return to the original governing concept of God the Creator, which is the kingdom concept.

The world needs a benevolent King. We have that King; we just don't recognize Him. Once we are under the rule of this gracious, merciful, benevolent, loving, caring King, He takes personal responsibility for us, not as servants or serfs, but as family and royal children. History continually fails to show us a government that manifests the equality, harmony, stability, and community that man desires. In a true ideal kingdom, all the citizens' welfare is the personal responsibility of the king. This is why the original kingdom concept, as in the Kingdom of God taught by Jesus Christ, is superior to all other governments.

The concept of "commonwealth" describes the nature of the relationship the king has with his citizens and subjects. The wealth in a kingdom is common. In a true ideal kingdom there is no discrimination or distinction between the rich and the poor, for in such a kingdom all citizens have equal access to kingdom wealth and resources provided by the benevolent king. In essence, the king's interest is the welfare of the kingdom and everything in it.

(Excerpt: *Kingdom Principles*, Chapter 2)

QUESTIONS

1. In your opinion, how should we return to the governing concept of God the Creator? How will the kingdom concept be a part of our return?

2. Why do you believe we need a benevolent King but do not recognize that He is already here? How does His benevolence affect your life?

3. Do you feel that you are the personal responsibility of God the Creator? Why or why not? How can you increase in the realization of His benevolence toward you?

4. What does the "commonwealth" principle of the kingdom mean to you personally? How does this principle eliminate discrimination? How does it eradicate distinction?

5. What does it mean that the "king's interest is the welfare of the kingdom and everything in it"? Why is God so interested in us? How does this interest show the difference between a religious person and one who has a relationship with the King?

MEDITATION

"The care of the citizens by the king is a concept called 'kingdom welfare' and describes the king's personal commitment to look after the needs and wants of his citizens within his land. The word welfare can only be understood fully in the context of a kingdom. Whenever we submit to a king and his kingdom, we come under his welfare. Welfare is not a word that can be used in a democracy."

Think about the fact that you are "on welfare"—Kingdom welfare! In what ways have you experienced the welfare of the Kingdom? Take time to thank God for His care for you.

The Original Kingdom Concept

So God created man in His own image, in the image of God He created him; male and female He created them. God blessed them and said to them, "Be fruitful and increase in number; fill the earth and subdue it. Rule over the fish of the sea and the birds of the air and over every living creature that moves on the ground" (Genesis 1:27-28).

TODAY'S DEVOTION

Every person on earth, without exception, is seeking a kingdom. The kingdom concept of government is far superior to any governmental system devised by man. The caveat, of course, is that such a kingdom be ruled by a righteous and benevolent king. Otherwise, a kingdom will be no better than any other system.

The inherent superiority of a kingdom over other systems of government is an especially difficult concept for many people in the West. Few Westerners have ever lived under a kingdom and thus know little or nothing of how one operates. This difficulty is even more acute for citizens of the United States whose nation, after all, was established in rebellion against a kingdom.

Nevertheless, a kingdom ruled by a sovereign, righteous, and benevolent king remains the best system of government. The reason is simple: *The kingdom concept is of heavenly, not earthly, origin.* Its appearance on earth is due to another concept that originated in Heaven—the concept of *colonization*. Simply stated, *colonization is Heaven's system for earthly influence.*

Genesis 1:26-28's colonial charter delineated the purpose and defined the parameters of the colony. It also designated the persons who received responsibility for carrying out the King's desire.

(Excerpt: *Kingdom Principles*, Chapter 3)

QUESTIONS

1. Why do you think every person on earth seeks a kingdom? What does a kingdom offer that makes us desire it?

2. What makes the kingdom concept of government superior to other systems? What is the stipulation needed to make it superior? What are the characteristics you would see to identify a righteous and benevolent king?

3. What questions do you have about how kingdoms operate? How do your ideas about democracy conflict with the concepts of a kingdom?

4. What are the benefits of a kingdom ruled by a righteous and benevolent king? In your opinion, are there ways in which this type of government could be superior to democracy?

5. How would you explain colonization as a system from Heaven to influence the earth? Who is to carry out this colonization? Where is colonization to be conducted? Why?

246 Understanding Your Place in GOD'S KINGDOM Devotional Journal

---

MEDITATION

"God's original intent was to extend His heavenly government over the earth, and His plan for accomplishing this was to establish a colony of Heaven on the earth. ...By creative right, the earth is Heaven's crown land. ...God gave us rulership, not ownership. ...We are merely aliens and stewards of God's property."

Did God give the earth to us or did He give us dominion over His earth? Knowing that you are not the owner of anything on this planet can give you a new perspective into your role in its care and the use of its resources. In what ways?

God's Colonial Intent

...He who created the heavens, He is God; He who fashioned and made the earth, He founded it; He did not create it to be empty, but formed it to be inhabited... (Isaiah 45:18).

TODAY'S DEVOTION

We must understand the concept of colonization or else it will be impossible to fully grasp the essence of the Bible's message. A colony is "a group of emigrants or their descendants who settle in a distant land but remain subject to the parent country."1

As citizens of Heaven, we inhabit the earth for the purpose of influencing it with the culture and values of Heaven and bringing it under the government of the King of Heaven.

His purpose in colonizing earth was to show the spiritual powers of darkness how beings created in His own image could be planted on the earth and bring in the government and culture of Heaven so that in the end, the earth would look just like Heaven.

God's government, the government of Heaven, is a kingdom, and God is the King. God "invented" the kingdom concept and established it first in Heaven.

Once His Kingdom was established in Heaven, God chose this planet specifically as the location of His Kingdom colony. Then He placed on it human beings created in His image to run the colony for Him. The first earthly kingdom was merely an extension of His Kingdom in Heaven.

(Excerpt: *Kingdom Principles*, Chapter 3)

---

1.   "Colony," *Nelson's Illustrated Bible Dictionary* (Nashville: Thomas Nelson Publishers, 1986).

QUESTIONS

1. Why do you think the concept of colonization is so important to understanding the message of the Bible? How does this concept affect our view of Christianity?

2. How do you influence the earth with the culture and values of Heaven? Are there ways that you help bring the earth under the government of the King of Heaven?

3. Why does our ability to fulfill our mandate to colonize the earth affect the spiritual powers of darkness? What affect do you think you have?

4. What do you know of the Kingdom of Heaven in terms of its government? How does our planet reflect that Kingdom? How does it not reflect Heaven's government?

5. If the earth is merely an extension of God's Kingdom in Heaven, how must we demonstrate God's Kingdom to those who do not know Him?

MEDITATION

"Human kingdoms had citizens who were subject to the king's personal ambitions, goals, whims, and desires. God's Kingdom is different. In the Kingdom of God there are no subjects, only citizens — but every citizen is a king (or queen) in his or her own right. This is why God is the King of kings. He is the High King of Heaven who rules over the human kings He created to rule over the earthly domain."

Take time to consider how God has made you to be a king or queen on this earth. How does your rulership reflect the High King of Heaven's rulership?

DAY 10

The Kingdom Is Here

I will put enmity between you and the woman, and between your offspring and hers; He will crush your head, and you will strike His heel (Genesis 3:15).

252   Understanding Your Place in GOD's KINGDOM Devotional Journal

TODAY'S DEVOTION

Adam and Eve's rebellion cost them their kingdom. With Adam and Eve's abdication, lucifer seized control of their earthly domain as a brazen, arrogant, and illegal pretender to the throne.

Immediately the King of Heaven put in motion His plan to restore what man had lost...a *kingdom*. Adam and Eve did not lose a religion because they had never had a religion; they had a kingdom. Religion is an invention of man, born of his efforts to find God and restore the kingdom on his own. But only God can restore the kingdom man lost.

The first words of Jesus' ministry were an announcement of the arrival of the Kingdom. This was the only message Jesus preached. Everything He said and did related to the Kingdom and its arrival on earth.

Jesus said, *"Repent"* (which means to change your mind or adopt a new way of thinking), *"for the kingdom of heaven is **near**"* (which means, in effect, that it has arrived). When Jesus brought the Kingdom of Heaven to earth, He brought also the promise of restoring to humankind the dominion over the earth that Adam and Eve had lost in Eden. He brought back our rulership.

(Excerpt: *Kingdom Principles*, Chapter 3)

QUESTIONS

1. What do you imagine Adam and Eve's kingdom was like before they sinned? When they abdicated their rule, who took over for Adam and Eve? Why is his throne illegal?

2. Why do you think God wants to restore to us what was lost in the Garden of Eden? Have you seen this process of restoration in your life and in the lives of those around you?

3. "Adam and Eve did not lose a religion because they had never had a religion; they had a kingdom." What does this mean to you? How is a religion a dead end while a kingdom promises eternity?

4. Why is the source of kingdom restoration so important to the success of God's purpose for earth? When man tries to restore the kingdom, what is the result?

5. By looking at Jesus' example, what do we see about the importance of the Kingdom of God to us? How does His example show you what purpose you have in colonization and how you are to conduct Kingdom business?

MEDITATION

"Before we could be fully restored to our Kingdom, the matter of our rebellion against God had to be dealt with. Jesus' death paid the price for our rebellion so that we could be restored to a right standing with our King, and be reinstalled in our rightful place as rulers of the earthly domain. The Cross of Christ is about Kingdom restoration of power and authority. It is about regaining rulership, not religion."

Take time to thank God for your right standing with Him because of the blood of Jesus. Pray about your rightful place as a ruler of the earthly domain. How do you define your rulership and not your religion?

Sons and Daughters, Not Servants

But when the time had fully come, God sent His Son, born of a woman, born under law, to redeem those under law, that we might receive the full rights of sons (Galatians 4:4-5).

TODAY'S DEVOTION

The King of Heaven wants sons and daughters, not servants. Religion produces servants. It revels in the spirit of servitude. Sons and daughters of the King see service as a privilege; religious people see it as an obligation.

Jesus came that we might "receive the full rights of sons." This is legal language. They refer to *legal* rights and entitlements based on relationship of birth. We are sons and daughters of God. Sonship is our right by creation. Christ did not die to improve us; He died to regain and confirm us. The price He paid was not to make us worthy but to prove our worth. He did not come to enlist an army of servants. He came to restore the King's sons and daughters to their rightful position—rulership as heirs of His Kingdom.

If we are heirs and are destined to rule in our Father's Kingdom, then we had better learn to understand His Kingdom and how it operates. We must learn how to think, talk, and live like Kingdom citizens. The Kingdom is the most important message of our age and the answer to the dilemma of ancient and modern man.

(Excerpt: *Kingdom Principles*, Chapter 11)

QUESTIONS

1. Describe the difference between a servant who serves and a son or daughter of the King of Heaven who serves. How can you tell the difference as you watch people serve in the world around you?

2. Why would the world see "service as a privilege" as being illogical according its concepts of serving? How can we change how the world views service?

3. Have you received your entitlement? What does this mean to you? To what are you entitled?

4. Explain the role Christ's death had in the lives of sons and daughters of the King of Heaven. How does His death become more meaningful in this life when we see what His work accomplished for our relationship with God?

5. What do you think it means to "think, talk, and live" like Kingdom citizens? Of these three, what is easiest for you to do? What needs the most work?

MEDITATION

*"According to Jesus Christ, everyone is trying all
they can to find it and forcing their way through
life to lay hold on it:*

*Since that time, the good news of the kingdom of God is being
preached, and everyone is forcing his way into it* (Luke 16:16b).

*Everyone of the over six billion people on earth are
searching for this Kingdom."*

Consider Luke 16:16b and your experience. In what ways do
you see people forcing their way through life to lay hold of the
Kingdom?

Understanding the Kingdom Concept of Kings

"Now if you obey Me fully and keep My covenant, then out of all nations you will be My treasured possession. Although the whole earth is Mine, you will be for Me a kingdom of priests and a holy nation." These are the words you are to speak to the Israelites (Exodus 19:5-6).

TODAY'S DEVOTION

It has been a popular notion to celebrate the opposition against monarchies, and many have even suggested the eradication of the concept of monarchies from our so-called modern or post-modern world. However, many of the democracies in our world today are also plagued with the same defects and shortcomings. In essence, the problem is not the king, the kingdoms, or even the form of government, but the defects in the human nature that functions in any of these systems.

Yet the kingdom concept is the only one presented, preached, promoted, taught, and established by Jesus Christ. His proposed solution to mankind's problems on the earth is the establishment of the Kingdom of Heaven in the earth. The message of the Bible and the focus of Jesus was not a religion or, for that matter, any of the many subjects we have magnified and many have preached as "the gospel" or good news to the world. For instance, Jesus never preached as a priority public message subjects like faith, prosperity, giving, deliverance, or even His death on the Cross or resurrection as "the gospel." But He repeatedly promoted and declared "the Kingdom of God and Heaven" as His principal message.

(Excerpt: *Kingdom Principles*, Chapter 4)

QUESTIONS

1. Consider the author's statements about our reaction to monarchies and democracy. Have you been biased against monarchies based on your experience with democracy?

2. What defects in human nature bring about problems in any form of government? Do these defects show themselves even in the "government" within businesses, ministries, or even the family?

3. Have you ever thought about the fact that Jesus never preached about democracy? Why do you think He only preached about the kingdom concept?

4. How did Jesus speak of the Kingdom as the "gospel"? When we think about His public messages, on what do His parables center?

5. Jesus used illustrations, stories, parables, sermons, and even healings to demonstrate the Kingdom. What are some of things you can use to demonstrate the Kingdom in your arena of relationships?

MEDITATION

"I am well aware that what I have shared about monarchies and democracies may be cause for much reaction, mental conflict, and religious resistance; but I would encourage you to search and research the four Gospels for yourself and discover this surprising reality. Jesus also indicated that this message of the 'Kingdom' would be His disciples' message to their world."

Take some time to scan the Gospels for references to the Kingdom of God. Highlight these and make note of any changes in your way of thinking about a kingdom.

Jesus Was Kingdom Focused

He replied, "The knowledge of the secrets of the kingdom of heaven has been given to you, but not to them" (Matthew 13:11).

TODAY'S DEVOTION

Jesus' message was clearly kingdom focused and not religiously motivated:

Our Father in heaven, hallowed be Your name, Your kingdom come, Your will be done on earth as it is in heaven (Matthew 6:9b-10).

But seek first His kingdom and His righteousness, and all these things will be given to you as well (Matthew 6:33).

And I confer on you a kingdom, just as My Father conferred one on Me (Luke 22:29).

"You are a king, then!" said Pilate. Jesus answered, "You are right in saying I am a king. In fact, for this reason I was born, and for this I came into the world, to testify to the truth. Everyone on the side of truth listens to Me" (John 18:37).

These statements show and emphasize the preoccupation Jesus had with the kingdom concept rather than a religion. Note in particular the last statement above, where Jesus declares Himself a "king" and not a president or prime minister or mayor. This is why it is necessary and essential that we rediscover and desire to understand the Kingdom as a concept and a reality. It is the foundation of God's plan for mankind.

(Excerpt: *Kingdom Principles*, Chapter 4)

QUESTIONS

Reference	Key Words	What This Means to Me	About the Kingdom
Matthew 6:9-10			
Matthew 6:33			
Luke 22:29			
John 18:37			

From the chart above, what have you discovered about God's Kingdom?

MEDITATION

"The original ideal kingdom concept is distinct from the earthly version even though it contains many of the same components and concepts of all kingdoms. Why did God choose a kingdom and not a republic, a democracy, or socialism? What are the benefits of being in a kingdom over a democratic republic or a communistic regime or socialist form of government? Why is Jesus a King and not a president?"

From what you have learned and experienced, what would your answers be to the above questions? Pray that God would give you the proper perspective of His Kingdom on earth and your role in it.

Sovereign Rule

Jesus said, "My kingdom is not of this world. If it were, My servants would fight to prevent My arrest by the Jews. But now My kingdom is from another place" (John 18:36).

TODAY'S DEVOTION

A kingdom is the sovereign rulership and governing influence of a king over his territory, impacting it with his will, his intent, and his purpose, manifesting a culture and society reflecting the king's nature, values, and morals.

The very heart of any kingdom is its king. Heaven exists because of the creative activity of God. It is infused with His presence, character, and authority.

Jesus came to the earth to reestablish the Kingdom. The Bible leaves no doubt as to His Kingship.

Jesus said, "My kingdom is not of this world," and "My kingdom is from another place," clearly implying that He was a King. He was speaking of the Kingdom of Heaven. Notice that Jesus said that His Kingdom was not *of* or *from* this world; He never said that it was not *in* this world. His Kingdom on earth originated in Heaven.

God created us for kingship—for dominion—and inside each of us is a latent kingdom consciousness striving for expression. This consciousness reveals itself in various ways, such as in our natural resistance to being ruled or controlled by any other person and our continual longing to control the circumstances of our own lives.

(Excerpt: *Kingdom Principles*, Chapter 4)

QUESTIONS

1. How do you see God's sovereign rulership in the government of your own life choices and mind-set? How does His will, intent, and purpose manifest itself in the culture of your local church?

2. What earthly monarch can you think of who was considered to be a kind and benevolent king or queen? Can you think of one who was considered a tyrant? How did these nations receive their identity from their leaders?

3. How has Jesus reestablished the Kingdom on earth? How does His Kingship define the Kingdom that He reestablished?

4. Where is the source of the Kingdom on earth? How did Jesus bring Heaven to earth? How are we supposed to do the same?

5. Do you feel that you have a "natural resistance to be ruled or controlled by any other person"? Do you feel that you have a longing to control your own circumstances? What does the knowledge of why you have these feelings do to bring perspective to these feelings?

MEDITATION

"We all seek power over things and over circumstances, and that is what the Kingdom of Heaven promises. Jesus said, 'I will testify to the truth of the Kingdom, and when you hear Me, what I have to say will resonate with the kingdom consciousness that is already in you.' We connect with the Kingdom message because it addresses the most deep-seated longing of our heart—our longing to be kings."

Take time to think about the drive within you that seeks to have power over circumstances and things. How does this drive relate to your longing to be a king?

DAY 15

The King Is Central to His Kingdom

When Jesus had finished saying these things, the crowds were amazed at His teaching, because He taught as one who had authority, and not as their teachers of the law (Matthew 7:28-29).

TODAY'S DEVOTION

If we want to be prepared to resume our rightful place as kings, then we had better learn what it means to be a king and how a king relates to his kingdom.

The first thing we need to understand is that *a king is the central component of his kingdom*. A king embodies the essence of his kingdom; the kingdom is the king. Without the king, there is no kingdom. In a kingdom, the king is the constitution. His word is the law. His word is the government.

Second, *a king is the ultimate and only source of authority in his kingdom*. In the Kingdom of Heaven, the authority of God the King is exclusive and absolute. His word is law and His will is carried out even to the farthest reaches of His realm. And God's realm is infinite.

Third, *the sovereignty of a king is inherent in his royal authority*. The people do not make a king sovereign; he is born sovereign. As sovereign, a king is free to do as he pleases with no accountability to anyone else in the kingdom. Otherwise, a king has no true authority. He is completely self-determining.

(Excerpt: *Kingdom Principles*, Chapter 4)

QUESTIONS

1. What do you think it means to be a king in God's Kingdom on earth? What characteristics would you have? How would you make decisions?

2. What do you think it means when the author says, "Without the king there is no kingdom"? Explain this in light of unbelievers on this earth.

3. What do you think it means when the author says that "the king is the constitution. His word is the law"? What does this mean in light of man-made laws that are not borne from the Kingdom of God?

4. How does the authority of God speak to the rebellion that is on the earth? How does God carry out His will in spite of rebellion?

5. How does the sovereignty of God answer questions of luck and victimization by circumstance? How do people hold God "accountable" for tragic natural disasters yet do not credit Him with supernatural blessings?

MEDITATION

"No one has the authority to tell God what to do. God's sovereignty is absolute. While this may seem restrictive, in many ways it actually relieves a lot of pressure. If you are under the King and someone asks you, 'What do you think about so-and-so?' you can defer to the King's authority: 'What I think does not matter. I am bound to follow my King, and my King says this....'"

Obviously, to answer questions correctly about the Kingdom, we need to know the words of the King in the Bible. Do you have a regular discipline of memorizing the Word of God? Pray about how you can implement a memorization program or continue one if you have it.

DAY 16

Fourteen Characteristics of a King: Part 1

The kingdom of the world has become the kingdom of our Lord and of His Christ, and He will reign for ever and ever (Revelation 11:15b).

TODAY'S DEVOTION

A king is distinct both from a democratically elected leader, such as a president or prime minister, as well as from a dictator in a totalitarian state. Following are 7 of 14 characteristics of a king that clarify that distinction. [The next journal entry will complete the 14 characteristics.]

1. **A king is never voted into power.** His power is inherent from birth.

2. **A king is king by birthright.** His kingship is not conferred by men. We do not make Him King; all we can do is acknowledge that He *is* King.

3. **A king cannot be voted out of power.** He was King before this world began, and He will still be King after it has passed away.

4. **A king's authority is absolute.** When the King speaks, He speaks with absolute authority.

5. **A king's word is law.** No one can countermand His orders, negate His pronouncements, set aside His decrees, or amend His statutes.

6. **A king personally owns everything in his domain.** A kingdom is the only form of government where the ruler owns everything and everyone.

7. **A king's decree is unchanging.**

Heaven and earth will pass away, but My words will never pass away (Matthew 24:35).

(Excerpt: *Kingdom Principles*, Chapter 4)

QUESTIONS

Fill out the chart below based on the seven characteristics above.

Characteristic of a King	Compare to Democracy	Compare to Your Church's Government	Your Notes/Comments
Never voted into power	President voted into office		

MEDITATION

The law of the Lord is perfect, reviving the soul. The statutes of the Lord are trustworthy, making wise the simple. The precepts of the Lord are right, giving joy to the heart. The commands of the Lord are radiant, giving light to the eyes. The fear of the Lord is pure, enduring forever. The ordinances of the Lord are sure and altogether righteous.... By them is Your servant warned; in keeping them there is great reward (Psalm 19:7-9,11).

"The King's word is law. Great reward follows obedience. Disobedience brings severe penalties."

List the benefits of the Lord's law (statutes, precepts, commands, ordinances). Spend time before the Lord embracing all these benefits.

Fourteen Characteristics of a King: Part 2

...All authority in heaven and on earth has been given to Me. Therefore go and make disciples of all nations... teaching them to obey everything I have commanded you. And surely I am with you always, to the very end of the age (Matthew 28:18-20).

TODAY'S DEVOTION

[This section is a continuation of the last journal entry, and it completes the 14 characteristics of a king.]

8. **A king chooses who will be a citizen.** The people do not vote for the King, but in essence, He votes for them.

9. **A king embodies the government of his kingdom.** The Kingdom of Heaven is here because the King of Heaven is in the hearts and lives of His citizens.

10. **A king's presence is the presence of his authority.** When the King shows up, His full authority is present. Kingdom citizens may always exercise kingly authority because the King is always present with them.

11. **A king's wealth is measured by his property.** The King of Heaven owns everything everywhere in both the natural and supernatural realms.

12. **A king's prosperity is measured by the status of his citizens.** A citizen of the Kingdom of Heaven automatically prospers because the King of Heaven is the wealthiest of all.

13. **A king's name is the essence of his authority.** Jesus the King has delegated His authority to His citizens. He promised to do anything that they asked in His name.

14. **A king's citizenry represents his glory.** Kingdom citizens are to reflect the character of their King, who is righteous, just, benevolent, compassionate, and full of glory.

(Excerpt: *Kingdom Principles*, Chapter 4)

QUESTIONS

Fill out the chart below based on the seven characteristics above.

Characteristic of a King	Compare to Democracy	Compare to Your Church's Government	Your Notes/Comments
Chooses who will be citizen	Citizens choose		

MEDITATION

"Kingdom citizens are to reflect the nature and
character of their King, who is righteous, just,
benevolent, compassionate, and full of glory.
This is why there is no poverty in the Kingdom
of Heaven, no economic crisis, and no shortages.
As King David observed:

The Lord upholds the righteous. …I was young and now I am old,
yet I have never seen the righteous forsaken or their children beg-
ging bread (Psalm 37:17b, 25).

How well do you reflect the nature and character of your King?
Do people see you as someone who is righteous, just, benevolent, compassionate, and full of glory?

Understanding the Kingdom Concept of Lord

For God is the King of all the earth; sing to Him a psalm of praise. God reigns over the nations; God is seated on His holy throne. The nobles of the nations assemble as the people of the God of Abraham, for the kings of the earth belong to God; He is greatly exalted (Psalm 47:7-9).

TODAY'S DEVOTION

The concept of lord is one of the fundamental principles of a kingdom. It is this quality of lordship that distinguishes a king from a president, a prime minister, a mayor, and a governor. Lordship makes a king unique.

All kings are automatically lords. *King* relates to *dominion*, while *lord* relates to *domain*. The word *dominion* refers to a king's authority—his power; the word domain refers to the territory over which his authority extends. A king exercises authority (dominion) over a specific geographical area (domain) and within that area his authority is absolute.

Kingship has to do with authority, and lordship has to do with *ownership*. *All true kings must have **and own** territory.* This is the kingdom lordship principle.

As lord, a king literally and legally owns everything in his domain. If the king owns everything, then no one in the kingdom owns anything. If the king owns everything, he can give anything to anyone at any time according to his own sovereign choice.

Because a king's dominion is so closely tied to territory, his wealth is measured by the size and richness of his domain. The larger and richer their domain, the greater their reputation and glory.

(Excerpt: *Kingdom Principles*, Chapter 5)

QUESTIONS

1. From your understanding of kingship thus far, why do you think lordship is such an important aspect of being king? How does lordship make a king unique?

2. What does kingship have to do with dominion and authority? What is God's dominion and authority? What is our dominion and authority?

3. What does lordship have to do with domain and ownership? What is in God's domain and ownership? What is in our domain and ownership?

4. What does this mean in terms of the life of Christians today: "If the king owns everything, then no one in the kingdom owns anything"? How does this principle work in your life?

5. What does this mean in terms of the life of Christians today: "If the king owns everything, he can give anything to anyone at any time according to his own sovereign choice"?

MEDITATION

1.   *"A king personally owns everything in his domain. There is no private ownership in a kingdom. Everything belongs to the king."*

2.   *"Use of anything in a kingdom is a privilege. If the king owns everything, then anything in that kingdom that we use is not by right but by a privilege granted by the king."*

Looking at the two principles of lordship above, what can you say about your relationship to your King and His relationship to you?

King and Lord

"The silver is Mine and the gold is Mine," declares the Lord *Almighty* (Haggai 2:8).

TODAY'S DEVOTION

The Bible, the constitution of the Kingdom of Heaven, plainly identifies God as King and Lord of all. One of the most common Hebrew words used to refer to God in the Old Testament is Adonai, which literally means proprietor or owner. It is usually translated "Lord." The personal name for God, Yahweh, although difficult to translate with complete accuracy, carries the same idea of master, owner, or lord.

In the same way, the New Testament reveals Jesus Christ as Lord and Owner of all. The most common Greek word for "Lord," *Kurios*, is applied to Jesus repeatedly. *Kurios* signifies having power. It also means one who possesses ultimate authority; master. Everything the Old Testament says about God as Lord, the New Testament says about Jesus.

The Lordship of Jesus is also by creative rights and was a natural result of His role in the creation of all things both seen and unseen. In essence, we do not "make" Jesus Lord; He is Lord by creative right, whether we acknowledge Him or not. Jesus Christ is King and Lord of all.

(Excerpt: *Kingdom Principles*, Chapter 5)

QUESTIONS

1. "The Bible, the constitution of the Kingdom of Heaven..." — What aspects of the United States' Constitution are found within the pages of the Bible? How does the Divine Constitution bring legality to the Kingdom on earth?

2. When we give praise to God as "Adonai," what are we praising about Him? Why is this praise important to us as citizens of the Kingdom?

3. When we acknowledge Jesus Christ as "Kurios," what are we acknowledging about Him? Why is this important to us as believers?

4. Since Jesus Christ is your Owner, are there aspects of His ownership that are restricting? Are there aspects of His ownership that are liberating?

5. Why can't we "make" Jesus Lord? When we discover His Lordship, what are we saying about His rights? What are we saying about our rights?

MEDITATION

1. *"A king can give or distribute anything to anyone in his kingdom. Because he owns it, He can shift things around any way he pleases. We need to hold onto 'our' possessions lightly."*

2. *"Submission to a king's lordship means that we have no right to ourselves. The moment we say 'Jesus Christ is Lord,' we acknowledge that we have no more right to our own life; it now belongs to Christ."*

Looking at the two principles of lordship above, what can you say about your relationship to your King and His relationship to you?

DAY 20

Living Under a Lord

If you confess with your mouth, "Jesus is Lord," and believe in your heart that God raised Him from the dead, you will be saved (Romans 10:9).

Lordship in a kingdom protects the citizenship from competition with their fellow citizens for national resources. It destroys such elements as jealousy, fear, deceit, and hoarding. Submission to a king as lord positions the citizen to receive from the king.

If you say, "Jesus is Lord," you are acknowledging His authority over you as well as your responsibility to obey Him. There is no such thing as lordship without obedience.

If Jesus is Lord, He must receive first priority in your life. He is above every other love, every other loyalty, every goal, dream, and ambition.

You cannot call Him *Lord* and then start making excuses for not obeying Him.

Living under a Lord also means giving up all concepts of personal ownership. This does not mean you have to give away all your personal possessions. We can enjoy these things as long as we remember who owns them.

In the Kingdom of Heaven, there is no economic crisis and there are no shortages. When we relinquish our sense of ownership and acknowledge God as the Owner and ourselves as stewards, we are now depending on Him for our welfare. And He is a benevolent and generous Lord.

(Excerpt: *Kingdom Principles*, Chapter 5)

QUESTIONS

1. Think about how the Lordship of Christ has protected you as a citizen of His Kingdom. Has it destroyed jealousy, fear, deceit, and hoarding in your life? Do you look to God for your resources?

2. How has the authority of the Lord worked on your behalf? How easy is it to obey the Lord? Are there areas that need improvement?

3. Have you given God, your Lord, first priority in your life? Are there things or relationships that try to crowd Him out of the number one spot?

4. Have you ever found yourself giving the Lord excuses for not obeying what He has said? Have you justified your sin because of pressure or circumstances? What should we do instead?

5. Does the idea of not having any personal ownership in the Kingdom bother you at any time? How does trusting God for His resources have a counterbalance in knowing they are His resources and not yours?

MEDITATION

1.   *"Obedience is acknowledgment of lordship. When we obey the King, we are saying, 'My life is Yours. Your wish is my command.'"*

2.   *"Thanksgiving is an acknowledgment of the King's Lordship. Daily thankfulness reveals that we believe that the King owns all and is the source of all we have."*

3.   *"The word 'Lord' can never be used with the word 'but.' Either He is Lord of all, or He is not Lord at all."*

Looking at the three principles of lordship above, what can you say about your relationship to your King and His relationship to you?

Understanding the
Kingdom Concept of Territory

In the beginning God created the heavens and the earth (Genesis 1:1).

Today's Devotion

E very kingdom must have territory. Because God is a King, and because a kingdom is a country ruled by a king and must therefore have territory, we can draw the conclusion that Heaven is a place. But the realm of the Kingdom of Heaven also takes in the natural world. God designed it this way when He created the earth and then fashioned man in His own image to rule it for Him.

Seven Kingdom Principles of Territory

Here are seven reasons why territory is so important to a king.

1. *No king can rule nothing.*

2. *There is no kingdom without a domain. The territory of a king is called his domain because he dominates it.*

3. *The essence of a kingdom is the right, the power, and the authority of the king to exercise complete sovereignty over a domain.*

4. *The heart of the kingdom concept is king domain.*

5. *A king is not a king without a domain. We are supposed to be rulers, but without our territory we cannot fulfill our destiny.*

6. *The wealth of a king's domain defines his value.*

7. *The loss of a domain is the loss of a kingdom.*

(Excerpt: *Kingdom Principles*, Chapter 6)

QUESTIONS

Outline the seven principles of territory above, using the chart to record your thoughts.

Principle	What does this mean to God's Kingdom on earth?	What does this mean to my rulership?
No king can rule nothing.		

MEDITATION

"God does not want to come here where we are personally, so that we can retain our authority as earthly kings. Jesus prayed that we would not be taken out of the world but be kept in it but away from evil. The earth is man's key to dominion power and his only legal territory for rulership."

What do these words mean to you and your rulership? Where are you to rule? Where are you not to rule? Do you live to rule now or are you waiting for Heaven? Why is this important to your Kingdom destiny?

Five Principles of Man's Earthly Authority

I tell you the truth, whatever you bind on earth will be bound in heaven, and whatever you loose on earth will be loosed in heaven (Matthew 18:18).

God created us to be kings over the earthly realm, and He will not rest until we are fully restored to our rightful place. Here are five principles that help explain the basis of our authority on earth as God intended it to be.

1. *The first thing God gave man was territory.* He did not give man a religion or rules to follow. He gave him land.

2. *The earth was created to give man kingship legitimacy.* God gave us the earth so that our kingship would be legal.

3. *The domain of earth is mankind's legal right, power, and authority of rulership.* When God said, "Let *them* have dominion," He transferred the legal rights to the earth to us.

4. *"Let them" are the key words in the transfer of authority from God to man.* God delegated authority to us because He wants us to experience rulership.

5. *Man's kingship is by privilege, not by creative right.* We are kings by delegation, not by creation. God gave us rulership but not ownership. Our rulership "charter" includes a *sense* of ownership because He gave us sovereignty within our earthly dominion.

(Excerpt: *Kingdom Principles*, Chapter 6)

QUESTIONS

1. Look at principle number one above. What territory does mankind occupy? What territory has God given to you?

2. Why does the earth legitimize mankind's kingship? How does this legality cancel satan's claim on the earth? How does it cancel the enemy's claim on your life?

3. How is rulership defined by mankind's legal right, his authority, and his power? Why do we need these three to have true dominion? Do you exercise these three areas of rulership in your own life?

4. When God transferred His authority to man, He already knew man would sin and abdicate rulership in the Garden of Eden. God knows that you sin, so why does He transfer His authority to you anyway?

5. In your opinion, what is the difference between "creative right" and "privilege"? As God's delegate, how well do you rule? Do you ever try to take ownership? What is the difference between ownership and a sense of ownership?

MEDITATION

*"The transfer of ruling authority over the earth from God to man has major implications for all of us regarding our daily circumstances and our relationship to our society and culture. Therefore, it is important that we understand it. God has given us authority over the earth. That means **we're in charge**. Whatever we say goes."*

What implications does the transfer of ruling authority from God to man have on your life personally? How should this concept affect the way we perceive our activity on earth?

Ten Principles of the Power of the Land

Blessed are the meek, for they will inherit the earth (Matthew 5:5).

TODAY'S DEVOTION

Here are ten principles of the power of land.

1. The first thing God gave man was land.

2. The first thing man lost was land. Having lost his dominion, man discovered that the earthly environment was now hostile.

3. The first thing God promised Abraham was land, not Heaven. Our dream is to go to Heaven; God's dream is for us to possess land.

4. Real wealth is in the land. That's why it's called real estate.

5. He who owns the land controls the wealth. Kingdom-minded people go after land.

6. True wealth is in the land. It almost always increases in value the longer you own it.

7. The meek will inherit the earth. "Meek" means "gentle" and "disciplined." They will inherit the earth—not Heaven.

8. Land is the only estate that is real. Real estate is the only property of lasting value that we can pass to our children.

9. *God considers the loss of land a curse.* Every time God cursed the Israelites for their rebellion, He took their land.

10. *The restoration of land is a blessing.* Land has power because without land there is no domain; without domain there is no king.

(Excerpt: *Kingdom Principles*, Chapter 6)

QUESTIONS

1. "Firsts" are important in the Bible because they set precedents for later verses. Look at the first three principles above. What firsts help you to learn the power that God assigns to land?

2. Wealth and land are almost synonymous. Why is this true? Look at principles four through six above. What conclusions can you make about where our major investment should be?

3. Why do you think the meek inherit the earth? What is it about meek people that causes God to make this promise? Would you consider yourself as being meek?

4. Why is any other investment besides real estate, not as secure or safe as land? If our children inherit our money, why is it still not of lasting value like inheriting land is?

5. The land was used as a tool for God to discipline the Israelites. Why do you think this was so important to them? Did God restore their land when they repented? How does land help define a king and his kingdom?

MEDITATION

"The Bible promises a full resurrection in which all Kingdom citizens will have a new body, a physical body of some sort, and will reign in the earth forever, just as God intended from the beginning. In the meantime, He wants us to practice rulership and dominion. We possess the authority to act in the name of our King and bring the influence of His will and desires over this earthly domain."

Can you imagine what it will be like to reign on the earth forever? What areas of rulership and dominion do you need to practice to prepare for your eternal reign?

Understanding the
Kingdom Concept of Constitution

For I know the plans I have for you…plans to prosper you and not to harm you, plans to give you hope and a future. Then you will call upon Me and come and pray to Me , and I will listen to you. You will seek Me and find Me when you seek Me with all your heart. I will be found by you… (Jeremiah 29:11-14).

TODAY'S DEVOTION

The heart of all nations, empires, and kingdoms is the constitution. In a republic, the constitution is the covenant the people make with themselves; then they hire, by vote, a governing body to keep that covenant for them and with them. In a kingdom, the constitution is the king's covenant with his citizens. In a republic, the constitution is produced by the aspirations of the people, while in a kingdom the constitution is initiated by the king and contains his aspirations and desires for his citizens.

A constitution is established by whomever exercises power. In a kingdom all power resides in the king. The king's constitution is the documented will, purposes, and intent of the king. It expresses his personal desires for his kingdom and sets out the principles under which the kingdom will operate as well as the manner and conditions of how the king will relate to his people and they to him. A kingdom constitution is stamped with the essence of the nature, character, and personality of the king. This is why it is always good to have a king who is righteous, benevolent, and compassionate, with a genuine concern for the welfare of his citizens.

(Excerpt: *Kingdom Principles*, Chapter 7)

QUESTIONS

1. Think through the differences between a kingdom's constitution and a republic's constitution. What is the source? What are the perimeters? How is the constitution maintained? What kind of trust is invested in each and in whom?

2. If you were to choose how to run an earthly government, which would you choose? If you were God Almighty, why would you choose the kingdom constitution over a republic constitution?

3. Where does the power lie in executing a republic's constitution? What safeguards are there to keep a republic's constitution maintained?

4. Where does the power lie in executing a kingdom's constitution? What safeguards are there to keep a kingdom's constitution maintained?

5. What kind of trust and faith is inherent in keeping a kingdom's constitution working well? What kind of trust and faith is needed on the citizens' part? What kind of trust is needed on the king's part?

MEDITATION

*"In a kingdom, the constitution is **a royal contract** that the king has with his subjects. It is **not** the contract that the citizens have with the king. This is a very important distinction. A royal contract originates completely and exclusively in the heart, mind, and will of the king. His citizens have no input concerning the terms or conditions of the contract. Such unilateralism on God's part is an expression of His sovereignty."*

What is comforting about knowing that the King of kings has made a royal contract with you? What safety and security does it provide? Do you feel slighted in any way because you have not had any input into the contract?

The King's Will and Testament

Your word, O Lord, is eternal; it stands firm in the heavens (Psalm 119:89).

312 Understanding Your Place in GOD's KINGDOM Devotional Journal

TODAY'S DEVOTION

The constitution in a kingdom constitutes the expressed will of the king in tangible, written form. Putting the constitution in written form sets it up as a standard that can be measured easily as well as making its terms and conditions clear to everyone. The Bible is the expressed will of the King in written form. It is the constitution of His Kingdom.

The constitution is the will and the testament of the king for his citizens. *Will* and *testament* are two different but related words that are both important. A *will* is what is in the mind of a person—his or her desire and intent. A *testament* is the physical documentation of a person's will, codifying his or her desire and intent in the form of a legal document.

The Bible is divided into two sections called the Old *Testament* and the New *Testament*. They comprise God's *documented* thoughts concerning His *expressed* will, desire, and intent for the human race.

The Word of God, written down and printed in the Bible, is the most powerful document we have. It is the constitution of the Kingdom of Heaven, the testament of the will of the King for His citizens.

(Excerpt: *Kingdom Principles*, Chapter 7)

QUESTIONS

1. We often speak about the will of God. What do you know about God's will in general terms? How did you learn about God's will?

2. Our experiences can only be measured against the constitution in Heaven. What is comprised in this constitution? How does it evaluate and explain our experiences on earth?

3. Have you ever had the intent to say something to someone, so you wrote a note to that person to tell them your thoughts? How did this written note allow the other person to know the thoughts and intents of your heart? How does this same principle work for God Almighty and the Bible?

4. If a testament can stand up to being contested in a courtroom, why do you think so many contest the biblical Testaments' veracity and validity? How do you know the documentation in the Bible is accurate?

5. By conceding that the Bible is a legal, written document of the heavenly King, how could many people find answers to their questions of rights and privilege, blessings and challenges?

MEDITATION

"A testament provides protection from the abuse of rights. It protects the rights of the beneficiaries of the will. How will your beneficiaries be protected and receive the benefits you desire for them unless your will is written down and documented legally? That is the purpose of a testament. A testament can be contested in a courtroom. There is no doubt as to what you meant."

Think about what Jesus' last will and testament might have been before He ascended to Heaven. You are His beneficiary. What did you receive? Why can't this will be contested, even by the powers of darkness?

Seven Principles of the Kingdom Constitution

But the plans of the Lord stand firm forever, the purposes of His heart through all generations (Psalm 33:11).

TODAY'S DEVOTION

In the Kingdom of Heaven, we do not have the privilege of tampering with the constitution. It is not our document; it is the King's.

1. *The source of the constitution is the king, not the citizens.* The Constitution of the United States begins with, "We the people..." whereas the constitution of God's Kingdom says, "I, the Lord...."

2. *The constitution contains the benefits and privileges of the citizens.* It spells out the advantages of being a Kingdom citizen as well as everything the citizens can expect from the King.

3. *The king obligates himself to the tenets of the constitution.* The Bible states that whatever God says, He will do, and whatever He promises, He will bring to pass.

4. *The constitution contains the rights established by the king for the citizens.* It sets forth the benefits and privileges accruing to Kingdom citizens, and delineates their rights.

5. *The constitution cannot be changed by the citizens—only by the king.*

6. *The constitution is the reference for life in the kingdom.* God's standards for life in His Kingdom are found throughout the Bible.

7. *The constitution contains the statutes of the kingdom.* Statutes are fixed, predictable standards.

(Excerpt: *Kingdom Principles*, Chapter 7)

QUESTIONS

1. Look at principle number two. What are some of the advantages of being a Kingdom citizen that you have found in the Bible? What are some of the expectations that the Bible says God has of Kingdom citizens?

2. Look at principle six. What are some of the standards that you have found in the Bible?

3. Look at principle six again. How are Kingdom citizens supposed to live? What are the values, the ethics, the moral code, and standards of behavior for citizens of the Kingdom, and where can they be found?

4. Look at principle seven. When it rains does the statute change? What if it snows? What if the temperature tops 100 degrees? If you spit on it, curse it, hate it, does the statute change? Is there any way that you can change a statute? Then why do we try at times to change them?

5. The constitution contains the statutes of the Kingdom. One time Jesus said these words: "Heaven and earth will pass away before My statutes change. I will move the heavens and the earth before I move My statutes" (see Luke 16:17; 21:33). Explain this in terms of your experience and understanding.

MEDITATION

"Who are we to dare to think that we have the right or the authority to change or set aside the statutes that the King of Heaven has set in place? Religious people can do that any time they want, because they are not really in the Kingdom. Kingdom citizens, however, cannot. Our constitution says, 'The word of the Lord stands forever' (1 Peter 1:25a)."

What motivates believers to want to change what God has set in place? Why do we often feel that our way is best? How often do you feel this way?

DAY 27

Understanding the Kingdom Concept of Law

It is written: "Man does not live on bread alone, but on every word that comes from the mouth of God" (Matthew 4:4).

TODAY'S DEVOTION

In any civil society, the "rule of law" is the bedrock of order and social justice. Human nature being what it is, laws are necessary to keep man's baser instincts and drives in check, protect public safety and decency, and preserve the moral order.

The "law of the Lord" revives our spirit, gives us wisdom, and fills us with joy. It enriches us with wealth much greater than earthly riches. It warns against danger and foolishness that could destroy our lives and places us on the path to "great reward."

If we allow it, the "law of the Lord" will nourish us thoroughly body, soul, and spirit.

Seven Principles of Law

1. *All creation was designed to function by inherent principles. Inherent means "built-in"; existent from the beginning.*

2. *These principles are called "natural law." Natural law has to do with laws concerning the nature of a thing.*

3. *Natural law is the standard for effective function of everything that God has created.*

4. *Laws are the key to successful existence and a guarantee of fulfillment of purpose.*

5. *Laws protect purpose.*

6. *The purpose for law is to protect the constitutional covenant.*

7. *Laws are the conditions of covenant.*

(Excerpt: *Kingdom Principles*, Chapter 8)

QUESTIONS

1. Why does law help us keep order and social justice? Do you allow God's law to "rule" you? Are there laws that you find difficult to obey or embrace?

2. How do laws help keep man's baser instincts or drives in check? What are some of these instincts or drives? Do you have any instincts or drives that contend against the law?

3. How does the "law of the Lord" revive our spirit? Where have you gained wisdom from the law of the Lord? How does the law of the Lord give us joy?

4. How does the law of the Lord enrich our lives with wealth that is beyond earthly wealth? How has your life been made richer by God's law?

5. Look at the seven principles above. How are each of these true in your own life?

MEDITATION

"We often think of laws as unpleasant and inconvenient demands that restrict our freedom and limit our options. In reality, laws are designed to free us to pursue unlimited options by providing a safe environment where we can live in peace, security, and confidence. True freedom is always circumscribed by boundaries, and laws define those boundaries. Within those boundaries we are free to thrive, prosper, and reach our full potential."

Do you think laws are unpleasant and inconvenient? Do you see them as demands that restrict our freedom and options? What does true freedom mean to you?

The King's Words of Law

"This is the covenant I will make with the house of Israel after that time," declares the Lord. "I will put My law in their minds and write it on their hearts. I will be their God, and they will be My people" (Jeremiah 31:33).

TODAY'S DEVOTION

L aws are built into the very fabric of creation. Everything in the natural realm operates according to inherent principles. The same is true of the spiritual realm. The Kingdom of Heaven is like any other government in the sense that it has laws to protect it and ensure that it operates according to God's intent. Laws establish God's Kingdom. And these laws were put in place long before the first human being arrived. And yet so often, we have the arrogance and the presumption to question God or challenge Him about His laws and the way He runs things.

Laws always carry consequences for violation. If you try to defy the law of gravity by stepping out of a second-story window, you are in for a painful shock—*if* you survive the fall! When we violate the law, we receive the due penalty. God doesn't have to judge us; the law carries its own built-in "judgment."

All laws established by the King of creation were made to determine how all the natural realm should function and how human beings should relate to God and to each other.

(Excerpt: *Kingdom Principles*, Chapter 8)

QUESTIONS

1. What are some of the laws of nature? Why do people so easily accept these but have trouble accepting the laws of the spiritual realm?

2. Why did God develop spiritual laws? What purpose do they serve? Why do you think we need to know these laws even though we are living in the natural realm?

3. What are some of the consequences of violating the laws of nature? What are some of the consequences for violating spiritual laws?

4. How does the law become our judge? How is the judgment built into the law?

5. What do God's laws say about how we are to relate to Him and to each other? How well do you follow these laws?

MEDITATION

"Whatever becomes accepted as a 'norm' in our society eventually becomes a 'law' of our society. God's laws are designed to prevent us from accepting and normalizing evil and assigning it the force of law in our society. This is the protective nature of laws. They prevent ideas and behaviors that are contrary to the constitution and the good of the state and the people from becoming a dominant influence."

Have you experienced the progression of a norm in our society becoming a law? What are some examples of good laws and examples of bad laws?

Natural Law Versus Written Law

The law of the Lord is perfect, reviving the soul. The statutes of the Lord are trustworthy, making wise the simple. The precepts of the Lord are right, giving joy to the heart. The commands of the Lord are radiant, giving light to the eyes (Psalm 19:7-8).

TODAY'S DEVOTION

God intended law to be natural. To understand the Kingdom of Heaven, it is important also to understand the distinction between natural law and written law.

First of all, written law is necessary only when natural law is absent. If we human beings were all law-abiding by nature, there would be no need for written law. Our rebellion against God destroyed the rule of natural law in our lives and made written law (as well as human government) necessary to protect society and restrain evil.

Second, the purpose for written law is to restore natural law to the conscience. Because of our rebellion against God, we lost our instinctive knowledge and understanding of natural law. Our consciences became corrupt and our likeness to our Maker became tarnished and distorted. Things that were natural in the beginning now became "unnatural."

Third, natural law is sometimes referred to as the "spirit of the law." This reflects God's desire for His laws, the standards of His Kingdom, to become the norms of our society.

Remember, earth is a colony of Heaven, and the laws of the King of Heaven should apply here as much as they do there. Laws produce society because they determine social relationships.

(Excerpt: *Kingdom Principles*, Chapter 8)

QUESTIONS

1. If "God intended law to be natural," why does it often feel so unnatural? What laws are unnatural or difficult for you?

2. Look at the three distinctions between natural law and written law. Note these below.

   • When is written law necessary?

   • What is the purpose of the written law?

   • How is the "spirit of the law" exercised?

3. What role does our conscience have in obeying the law? In what instances does it help us? Where does it fall short?

4. How can something that used to be "natural" become "unnatural"? Have you witnessed this happening in your city or nation?

5. How do laws produce society? What role do laws have in determining social relationships?

MEDITATION

*"Any nation is only as good as the laws it enacts.
Bad laws do not cause a nation's social, moral, and
spiritual decline. They merely reflect a decline that
is already underway. Laws mirror the condition
of the nation. This is why it is so important for
Kingdom citizens to regain our understanding of the
'spirit of the law'—natural law. Natural law is the
fundamental operating principle of the Kingdom
of Heaven."*

How do the laws of the Kingdom show the goodness of the
Kingdom of God? How have you experienced that goodness?

Understanding the Kingdom Concept of Keys

I will give you the keys of the kingdom of heaven; whatever you bind on earth will be bound in heaven, and whatever you loose on earth will be loosed in heaven (Matthew 16:18-19).

TODAY'S DEVOTION

In Matthew 16 Jesus says that upon the "rock" He will build His "church." The word church itself is a political rather than a religious term. The entire discussion about keys and about binding and loosing is not religious but political.

Jesus was saying, "Upon the 'rock' of your confession of who I am, I will build My *government*." Jesus established not a religion but a political force.

The *ecclesia* is a secret group entrusted with secret information critical for the operation of the Kingdom. This group will be so powerful that even the "gates of hades will not overcome it."

The "secret information" that Jesus gives us is the keys *of* the Kingdom, not the keys *to* the Kingdom. As Kingdom citizens, we are already in the Kingdom; we don't need the keys to it. We need the keys that will unlock the power of the Kingdom and make it work in our lives. Only Kingdom citizens have these keys.

We have access to a power that mystifies those who are not yet in the Kingdom. We are supposed to be living life at a level where we tap into resources that others cannot explain.

(Excerpt: *Kingdom Principles*, Chapter 9)

QUESTIONS

1. The author tells us that the word *church* used in Matthew 16 is a political term. Why do you think we have seen the church as a religious entity and not a political one? What do we need to do to change the church?

2. Why do you think Jesus was going to build the church upon Peter's confession and not Peter himself? What was that confession? Why is that confession so important?

3. Why does the author say that the church is a "secret group"? What secret do they have? How powerful is the secret information that they carry?

4. What is the difference between the keys *of* the Kingdom and the keys *to* the Kingdom? Why is this distinction so important to us?

5. Why hasn't the church accessed the power that they have to mystify unbelievers? Why do you think Christians don't tend to live at a level where we tap into resources that others cannot explain?

MEDITATION

"Our Father, the King of Heaven, has given us the Kingdom. It is ours. The moment we turn from our rebellion against God and place our trust in Christ to salvage us from the consequences of that rebellion, we become naturalized citizens of the Kingdom of Heaven, with all the rights, benefits, and privileges that come with it."

How do you appropriate your rights? How do you enter into the full enjoyment of your benefits and privileges? What are the keys that you use to effectively live in the Kingdom?

$$\boxed{\text{DAY 31}}$$

Knowledge of the Secrets

The knowledge of the secrets of the kingdom of God has been given to you (Luke 8:10a).

335

TODAY'S DEVOTION

The Kingdom of Heaven is not a secret society, but its keys have to be learned. A secret is anything that is not commonly known. Miracles fall into this category. Jesus walked on water, healed the sick, raised the dead, and many other "miraculous" things.

But to Jesus, none of these were miracles. He said, "These are no miracles; I'm just using keys. I know how to put them in the locks, and they are unlocking prosperity, unlocking healing, unlocking peace, unlocking authority. Watch Me and you will see how the Kingdom should work for you. My Father has given you the knowledge of the secrets of the Kingdom. I will teach you how to use the keys."

Jesus' ecclesia was going to do the same things He was doing—and more—because the Holy Spirit who would come after He was gone would teach them the keys of the Kingdom and how to use them. One significant key is embedded in this passage: the key to opening the "warehouse" of Heaven. The key that opens that lock is *prayer*—asking in *Jesus' name*—and *whatever* and *anything* we ask will be done.

(Excerpt: *Kingdom Principles*, Chapter 9)

QUESTIONS

1. What are the kinds of secrets Jesus has given to the Church? Are these secrets that we are supposed to keep to ourselves, or just secrets that others have not discovered yet? What do we need to do to raise their interest in these secrets?

2. Explain what miracles are from the secrets of the Kingdom perspective. How is an experience that is abnormal to us actually quite normal to the Kingdom of God?

3. What are some of the locks that you have seen opened with keys to the Kingdom? What was the key that opened each lock respectively?

4. How do you think you can learn to use the keys of the Kingdom? What do you need in order to be equipped to use the keys? Will you need training or experience, knowledge or faith?

5. How is prayer a key that unlocks the locks that will enable us to operate in the miraculous? Why is Jesus' name so important in prayer?

MEDITATION

*"Jesus left no doubt that the Kingdom was supposed
to work for His ecclesia just as it worked for Him, for
on the night before His death He told them:*

*I tell you the truth, anyone who has faith in Me will do what I
have been doing. He will do even greater things than these, because
I am going to the Father (John 14:12)."*

What is the Church doing that Jesus did on earth? What is the
Church not doing that Jesus did? What should you be doing
that Jesus did when He was on earth?

Seven Principles of Keys

If you hold to My teaching, you are really My disciples. Then you will know the truth, and the truth will set you free (John 8:31b-32).

TODAY'S DEVOTION

Once we know the principles behind keys, we can understand how they work in the Kingdom. These principles define the properties of keys.

1. *Keys represent authority.* If you possess a key to a place, it means you have authority in that place.

2. *Keys represent access.* A key gives you access to everything that key opens.

3. *Keys represent ownership.* Possession of a key gives you de facto ownership of whatever that key opens.

4. *Keys represent control.* If you possess the key to something, you control it.

5. *Keys represent authorization.* Authorization means to be given the authority to act in the name of whoever gave you the authority.

6. *Keys represent power.* Whoever gives you keys gives you power at the same time.

7. *Keys represent freedom.* When you have keys, you are free to go in and out.

The keys of the Kingdom are the keys to ultimate truth, the knowledge of which brings true liberty. Freedom comes in knowing the truth. Truth alone is not what sets you free. What sets you free is the truth you know. The keys of the Kingdom can bring you into the knowledge of the truth.

(Excerpt: *Kingdom Principles*, Chapter 9)

QUESTIONS

Look at the principles above that define the properties of keys and fill in the chart below.

Principle	Benefit	What This Means for Me
Keys	represent Possession of a Key = authority	

MEDITATION

*"When you possess the keys of the Kingdom of Heaven, you have ownership of Heaven on earth. Jesus said, **'Whatever you bind on earth will be bound in heaven, and whatever you loose on earth will be loosed in heaven.'** In other words, you own on earth whatever is going on in Heaven. This means that you should never judge how your life is going simply by your circumstances."*

How often do you find yourself judging how your life is going by your circumstances? How can you operate in whatever is going on in Heaven and not be bound by what you see on earth?

Seven Characteristics of Keys

Command those who are rich in this present world not to be arrogant nor to put their hope in wealth, which is so uncertain, but to put their hope in God, who richly provides us with everything for our enjoyment (1 Timothy 6:17).

TODAY'S DEVOTION

1. *Keys are laws.* They are fixed, reliable standards that never change. When used correctly, they always work.

2. *Keys are principles.* They operate under fixed laws.

3. *Keys are systems.* They are beyond the reach of those outside the Kingdom but Kingdom citizens have access to those systems and can bring their influence to bear in earthly situations.

4. *Keys activate function.* They activate Heaven so that we can fully enjoy our rights and privileges as Kingdom citizens.

5. *Keys initiate action.* When we know how to use the keys, we initiate action in Heaven.

6. *Keys are the principles by which the Kingdom of God operates.* They give us access to the blueprints so that we can appropriate the inner workings of the Kingdom of Heaven.

7. *Keys cannot be substituted by feelings, emotions, wishful thinking, or manipulation.* You can wish and feel and beg all you want, but without the right keys, you will still be locked out. Feelings don't open doors. Keys do.

In the world's system, you get ahead by killing, hurting, manipulating, using people, or stealing. In the Kingdom of Heaven, everything is reversed. This is the way God's Kingdom works.

(Excerpt: *Kingdom Principles*, Chapter 9)

QUESTIONS

1. Look at principle number one. Can you give an example from the Bible of a law that is a fixed, reliable standard that does not change? How can we know how to use this law correctly?

2. Look at principle three. Does the fact that Kingdom systems are beyond the reach of those outside the Kingdom help draw them in or not? If we don't operate with these keys, how can that hurt the message of the gospel?

3. Look at principle five. When we do not see something happen immediately in the natural, how can we be sure that we have activated something in Heaven?

4. Look at principle six. Why is the operation of a company or government just as important as the goals it sets? Why do we need to know how things work in Heaven?

5. Look at principle seven. Why do you think the human side of us relies on begging and manipulation when we know it can't work in Heaven? What parts of us must be submitted to the Lord before we can release these unproductive methods and trust in God's methods?

MEDITATION:

"Principles are established by the manufacturer. God knows what is best for us. Because of our fallen nature, we are dysfunctional, believing either that there is nothing wrong with us or that whatever is wrong we can fix ourselves. Counterintuitive wisdom leads us to understand that the principles under which the Kingdom operates, are also the keys to bringing the life, law, and culture of Heaven to earth, even when human logic says otherwise."

Since God is your manufacturer, are you still under warranty? Are you supposed to operate in accordance with the specifications He has set? Do you ever fight against those specifications?

Understanding the Kingdom Concept of Citizenship

But our citizenship is in heaven. And we eagerly await a Savior from there, the Lord Jesus Christ, who, by the power that enables Him to bring everything under His control, will transform our lowly bodies so that they will be like His glorious body (Philippians 3:20).

TODAY'S DEVOTION

Citizenship is the most valuable asset of a nation and is not easily given because of its power and impact. Citizenship is not membership. Religions function on membership, while nations and kingdoms function on citizenship. Citizenship is necessary for the validity and legitimacy of any nation. Not only that, but citizenship is the most sacred privilege of a nation.

Citizenship has great power as well as great privileges. That is why people are willing to risk their lives and cross borders to pursue the hope of citizenship.

All nations have citizens and require immigration status. The Kingdom of God is no different. Every Kingdom citizen today is a naturalized citizen. We emigrated from a foreign country—a *"dominion of darkness"* (see Col. 1:13)—where we had been "exiled" ever since Adam's rebellion.

The new birth makes us citizens of Heaven, but our citizenship begins *immediately*. The Kingdom has come.

You can never appropriate what you postpone. That's what you call "locking up the Kingdom of God." Religion keeps pushing the Kingdom away from people. That is why so many religious people live defeated, destitute, and frustrated lives. They believe they have to wait for their "reward."

(Excerpt: *Kingdom Principles*, Chapter 10)

QUESTIONS

1. Why do you think citizenship "is the most valuable asset of a nation"? What does citizenship do for the nation? What does it do for the people?

2. Why is citizenship not the same as membership? Explain the difference. What does your citizenship of your country mean to you? What does your citizenship of the Kingdom of Heaven mean to you?

3. Why is citizenship "the most sacred privilege of a nation"? What privileges do you have in the nation in which you live? What privileges do you have in the Kingdom of God?

4. What kind of power does citizenship exercise? What powers do you exercise in your citizenship within your country? What powers do you exercise in the Kingdom of God?

5. Why is it important that we understand the Kingdom of God is for today and our citizenship in that Kingdom is an immediate citizenship?

MEDITATION

*"When it comes to matters of citizenship, the Kingdom of God is no different from any other country. Once people learn about the Kingdom of God, they can't wait to get in! My experience has been that once people know about the Kingdom and see it modeled, they want it! Such is the **power** of the **lure of citizenship** in the Kingdom of Heaven."*

If citizenship in the Kingdom of Heaven is so exciting, why do we not see people clamoring to get into the churches? Why does the church as a whole seem to have so little impact on our culture? What might you do to change this pattern?

DAY 35

Dual Citizenship

My kingdom is not of this world. If it were, My servants would fight to prevent My arrest by the Jews. But now My kingdom is from another place (John 18:36).

Today's Devotion

Most governments on earth allow dual citizenship, where citizens of one country may hold simultaneously legal citizenship in another. It is no different with the Kingdom of Heaven. All Kingdom citizens are simultaneously citizens of the Kingdom of Heaven as well as citizens of the earthly nation of their birth or their naturalization. We don't give up our earthly citizenship when we become citizens of the Kingdom. We don't have to be in Heaven to benefit from heavenly jurisdiction. Our citizenship is constant, and the Kingdom government exercises jurisdiction over us wherever we are.

The Kingdom constitution says that we are *in* the world but not *of* the world. So all Kingdom citizens possess dual citizenship—in Heaven and on earth. That status will continue until the day when the present Heaven and earth passes away and the King re-creates them both.

Culture is a product of the language, ideals, and values of a people or a nation. Even though people cannot recognize us as Kingdom citizens by our outward appearance, our distinctive language, ideals, and values should give us away. Our culture should reflect and reveal our citizenship as being *in* the world but not *of* the world.

(Excerpt: *Kingdom Principles*, Chapter 10)

QUESTIONS

1. How are you holding dual citizenship between earth and Heaven? How does this dual citizenship work?

2. How does heavenly jurisdiction work in your life? How does this jurisdiction impact the jurisdiction of your earthly citizenship?

3. What does it mean to be "in the world but not of the world"? How does this concept mark the choices we are to make and the way in which we are to live?

4. How has culture impacted the church in a negative way? How should the culture of Heaven impact the church? Then, how can the church truly impact the culture of the earth?

5. How does your Kingdom culture impact those around you? Are there any ways God would want you to reveal your Kingdom citizenship through the way you lead your life?

MEDITATION

*"We cannot see the Kingdom of Heaven because it is invisible. The fact that the Kingdom of Heaven is invisible does not mean that it has no impact. If the Kingdom of God resides **within** its citizens, this means that all Kingdom citizens are invisible also. We bear no physical or outward signs that broadcast to the world, 'I'm a Kingdom citizen!' Our citizenship must become known in other ways."*

If the Kingdom of Heaven is here now, why can't we see it? Why isn't there more evidence of it all around us? How can you increase the evidence of the Kingdom in your own life so that others will see it?

DAY 36

Understanding the Kingdom
Concept of Culture

For as he thinketh in his heart, so is he: Eat and drink, saith he to thee, but his heart is not with thee (Proverbs 23:7 KJV).

TODAY'S DEVOTION

Culture encompasses many things. Once you understand the culture of a people, you understand the people. Everything that makes a nation a nation and a people a people is wrapped up in their culture.

Every country has *land*—territory. The culture will reflect the environment in which citizens live.

A second key component is *language*. Language is the key to unity and a key factor in a nation's culture.

All countries have *laws*, which reflect the culture of that nation and vice versa.

Every nation utilizes specific and unique *symbols* to represent it and to help inspire unity, patriotism, loyalty, pride of nation, and a strong sense of national identity.

All nations have a *constitution*, which is a cultural document, containing in codified form the laws, ideals, and values of who wrote it.

All nations have a *moral code*, which embodies the moral standards under which the people have agreed to live and by which they have chosen to govern themselves.

Finally, there are *social norms*. Social norms are standards of speech, thought, and behavior that are accepted by the wide majority of the people as right and proper.

All of these together comprise what we call *culture*.

(Excerpt: *Kingdom Principles*, Chapter 11)

QUESTIONS

1. How does the environment and territory in which you live on earth affect the culture around you? What is the land and environment of the Kingdom of Heaven?

2. How does language affect your community and culture? What is distinctive about the language of Heaven?

3. What laws and symbols are reflected in the area in which you live? What laws and symbols exemplify the Kingdom of Heaven?

4. What moral codes and standards exist in the area in which you live? What are some of the moral codes and standards that exist in the Kingdom of Heaven?

5. What are some of the social norms that exist in your community? What are some of the social norms that are reflected by the true citizens of the Kingdom of Heaven?

MEDITATION

*"Culture is also what lies at the very center of the great cosmic conflict between the Kingdom of God and the kingdom of darkness. And earth is the battleground. Proverbs 23:7 means that the way we think determines who we become. In this context, the heart is the **mind**. And the Kingdom of God is a kingdom of the heart. Therefore, the King of Heaven is battling for the minds of the creatures He created in His own image."*

Where is the battleground within you? What issues does your mind face that need victory? How does the victory over your mind affect your presentation of Kingdom culture to those around you?

DAY 37

Manifestations of Culture

...Love, joy, peace, patience, kindness, goodness, faithfulness, gentleness and self-control. Against such things there is no law (Galatians 5:22-23).

TODAY'S DEVOTION

Culture manifests itself in a number of ways.

1. **Values.** Our values reflect our character.

2. **Priorities.** Culture manifests itself in the things we regard as most important.

3. **Behaviors.** The way we behave reveals our culture; it's that simple.

4. **Standards.** These reveal whether we have a culture that indulges and encourages mediocrity or inspires excellence.

5. **Celebration.** Our culture is revealed in the things we celebrate as well as in the manner that we celebrate.

6. **Morality.** The level of our moral conscience and consciousness reveals the level of our culture.

7. **Relationships.** Our culture is revealed in how well we take care of each other.

8. **Ethics.** Is honesty our best policy, or is honesty our only policy?

9. **Social norms.** Whatever is regarded as normal in our society reveals our culture.

10. **Dress.**

11. **Foods.**

12. **Permits.** We reveal our culture by what we permit.

13. **Acceptance.** Our culture is defined by what we accept.

14. **Rejections.** Our culture manifests in what we reject.

15. **Distinctions.** What makes the Kingdom culture distinctive from the culture of the world?

16. **Quality standards.** God never does anything halfway, and neither should His children.

(Excerpt: *Kingdom Principles*, Chapter 11)

QUESTIONS

Using the list of manifestations of culture, determine those (if any) that are distinctive of your community, region, or nation and those that are distinctive of the Kingdom of Heaven.

Manifestation	Distinctive to Your Community	Distinctive to the Kingdom of God
Values		
Priorities		
Behavior		
Standards		
Celebration		
Morality		
Relationships		
Ethics		
Social Norms		
Dress		
Foods		
Permits		
Acceptance		
Rejections		
Distinctions		
Quality Standards		

MEDITATION

"As Kingdom citizens, we need to take our cue from our King because His attitudes and responses reveal Heaven's culture. Whatever makes Jesus angry should make us angry and whatever makes Him happy should make us happy. Whatever fills Him with joy should make us joyful also and whatever brings Him sorrow should grieve our spirits as well."

How do we get cues from the King? How does He let us know what His attitude and responses are? Be sure to make time for Him to lead you to discover more of these cues.

Understanding the Kingdom
Concept of Giving to the King

"You are right in saying I am a king. In fact, for this reason I was born…" (John 18:37b).

TODAY'S DEVOTION

Adam was created with certain unique qualities and characteristics that set him apart as distinct from all other creatures on the earth. One of these qualities was self-determination. Man possessed the ability to reason—to frame his own thoughts and ideas and to make his own decisions. In this he was like his Creator. He was endowed also with the capacity for face-to-face, one-on-one intimate fellowship with God, a privilege that no other creature on earth enjoyed.

The Creator gave Adam the earth as his domain. Through inappropriate use of his power of self-determination, Adam rebelled against God and lost his earthly kingdom. Man became a slave in his own domain.

But the gifts and calling of God are irrevocable (see Rom. 11:29). God's original plan and purpose were still in place. Man's destiny was to rule the earth, so he had to get his Kingdom back. When the time was right in history, the King of Heaven sent His Son to earth to reestablish Heaven's rule here. As a human as well as the Son of God, Jesus had the authority both to restore the Kingdom and to rule it as King. Kingship was His birthright.

(Excerpt: *Kingdom Principles*, Chapter 12)

QUESTIONS

1. How was self-determination an important quality for God to give His citizens? Why did God desire man to be able to frame his own thoughts and ideas and make his own decisions?

2. How is man's self-determination tied into his ability to have intimate fellowship with God? How is your will involved in your own intimacy with God?

3. Adam inappropriately used his power of self-determination. How has this affected all of mankind ever since? Do you think your own inappropriate use of self-determination has an impact on others?

4. What does Romans 11:29 mean to you personally? How has God gifted you in spite of your failures? How does this fact give you hope of God's gift to come?

5. What was the best gift God ever gave? How did this gift set man in the right place to rule earth once again?

MEDITATION

*"The coming of Jesus Christ as King demonstrates
an important characteristic of God: He is a **giver**. In
fact, His honor as King of Heaven demands a gift. As
God, He gives because it is His nature. As Kingdom
citizens, we give because we are like Him, created
in His image and likeness, and because giving is a
proper way to honor a king."*

Take time to praise God for being the Giver. Praise Him first
and foremost for giving Jesus Christ as a substitute for your
sins. Then praise Him for all that you have in this life and the
life hereafter.

DAY 39

The Six Royal Kingdom Principles of Giving

Give, and it will be given to you. A good measure, pressed down, shaken together and running over, will be poured into your lap. For with the measure you use, it will be measured to you (Luke 6:38).

Today's Devotion

1. The power of kings is displayed in their wealth.

2. The purpose for a king's wealth is to secure his reputation—his glory.

3. The glory of a king is his power to out-give another king.

4. Giving places a demand on the king's wealth.

5. Giving requires a response from the king.

6. Giving to a king attracts his wealth to the giver.

This is directly related to the concept of stewardship versus ownership. As long as we feel we own what we have, we tend to cling to it and hold it close to our chest. In that posture, it is impossible to receive more. On the other hand, when we approach the King open-handed with our things, not only can we lay them at His feet as a gift, but we are also in a posture to receive. Giving to the King attracts His wealth because He is a giver and is attracted to those who share a like spirit.

We can never out-give God. Give, and He will give abundantly and overflowing in return. It's a principle of His Kingdom. Besides, His reputation and glory are at stake.

(Excerpt: *Kingdom Principles*, Chapter 12)

QUESTIONS

1. Look at the six principles of royal giving listed above. How do each of these have an impact on your life?

2. What does the author mean by "stewardship versus ownership"? What are you a steward over for the Kingdom of God?

3. What are the problems with a mind-set of ownership to citizens of the Kingdom? How does this mind-set keep us from receiving more from our King?

4. Why does giving to the King attract His wealth? Have you experienced this firsthand?

5. Why can we never out-give God? How are His gifts more demonstrative than anything we can give?

MEDITATION

"This is definitely a characteristic of the King of Heaven. As owner of literally everything, God is the richest King that was, is, or ever will be. No one can out-give God. And He gives lavishly without regard to our merit or our ability to repay. Don't forget that Jesus assured us that it was His Father's pleasure to give us the Kingdom. And He did not demand that we make ourselves 'worthy' first."

How easy is it for you to believe in the bounty of God? How easy is it for you to appropriate the bounty He has given to you?

Seven Reasons to Give to the King

And none shall appear before Me empty-handed (Exodus 34:21b NKJV).

TODAY'S DEVOTION

1. Royal protocol requires that a gift must be presented when visiting a king.

2. The gift must be fitting for the king.

3. The gift reveals our value or "worth-ship" of the king. The quality of what we offer the King and the attitude with which we offer it reveal much more than our words do of the value or worthiness we attach to Him.

4. Worship demands a gift and giving is worship. "Worth-ship" is where we get "worship." To worship the King means to ascribe worth or worthiness to Him.

5. Giving to a king attracts his favor.

6. Giving to a king acknowledges his ownership of everything. Giving to a king is simply returning to him what is already his.

7. Giving to a king is thanksgiving. Gratitude expressed is in itself a gift. The ultimate and greatest gift the King wants from us is summed up in these words:

Love the Lord your God with all your heart and with all your soul and with all your strength (Deuteronomy 6:5).

Giving activates royal obligation. Give Him *your* life and receive *His* life...remembering that *"It is more blessed to give than to receive"* (Acts 20:35).

(Excerpt: *Kingdom Principles*, Chapter 12)

QUESTIONS

1. Looking at the seven principles of giving above, what "rules" do you see for giving within the Kingdom of God?

2. Looking at the seven principles of giving above, what benefits do you see for citizens of the Kingdom?

3. Looking at the seven principles of giving above, how well do you observe these principles? What are the easiest to understand and follow? What are the most difficult to follow?

4. What does Deuteronomy 6:5 mean to you personally in terms of how you love the Lord your God? What does this verse mean in regards to keeping your mind, heart, soul, and strength preserved as gifts for your King?

5. What does it mean to give "Him your life and receive His life"? What does it entail to give Him your life? What kind of life does God give in return?

376 Understanding Your Place in God's Kingdom Devotional Journal

MEDITATION

"Giving is natural for kings and we too are kings."

1. If we all are kings, then we should give to each other.

2. When we give to the Body, we give to Christ the King.

3. Every time we meet one another, giving should be automatic.

4. The wise men knew there was a greater King on earth.

5. When you give to a king, you make a demand on what he possesses."

Looking at the five reasons of giving above, how well do you give? Ask the Lord to help you in any area of weakness you have toward giving.

Myles Munroe International

The Diplomat Center

P.O. Box N-9583
Nassau, Bahamas
Tel: 242-461-6423

Website: www.mylesmunroeinternational.com
Email: mmi@mylesmunroeinternational.com

For Information on Bahamas Religious Tourism

Tel: 1-800-224-3681
Website: worship.bahamas.com

In the right hands, This Book will Change Lives!

Most of the people who need this message will not be looking for this book. To change their lives, you need to put a copy of this book in their hands.

> *But others (seeds) fell into good ground, and brought forth fruit, some a hundred-fold, some sixty-fold, some thirty-fold* (Matthew 13:8).

Our ministry is constantly seeking methods to find the good ground, the people who need this anointed message to change their lives. Will you help us reach these people?

> *Remember this—a farmer who plants only a few seeds will get a small crop. But the one who plants generously will get a generous crop* (2 Corinthians 9:6).

EXTEND THIS MINISTRY BY SOWING
3 BOOKS, 5 BOOKS, 10 BOOKS, OR MORE TODAY,
AND BECOME A LIFE CHANGER!

Thank you,

Don Nori Sr., Founder
Destiny Image
Since 1982